The Cruise of
The Kate

The Cruise
of
The Kate

E. E. MIDDLETON

Introduction by Arthur Ransome

GRANADA
London Toronto Sydney New York

Granada Publishing Limited
8 Grafton Street, London W1X 3LA

First published 1870
This edition published by Granada Publishing 1984

British Library Cataloguing in Publication Data

Middleton, E. E.
    The cruise of the Kate.
    1. Kate (*Ship*)   2. England——
    Description and travel
    I. Title
    914.2'04286   DA625

ISBN 0-246-12310-9

Printed in Great Britain by
Billing & Sons Ltd., Worcester

THE CRUISE OF "THE KATE"

IS DEDICATED TO MY SISTER

KATE MIDDLETON

AFTER WHOM THE YACHT

WAS NAMED

CONTENTS

MAPS

EMPSON EDWARD MIDDLETON

BY ARTHUR RANSOME

WHEN in 1930 Sir Arthur Underhill wrote a short history of The Royal Cruising Club, which he had founded fifty years before, he mentioned *The Cruise of The Kate* as one of the three books that had shared in making cruising in salt waters his lifelong recreation.

There are several reasons why a reprint of it should be welcomed, and of these the first is that it is an account of a modest voyage round our own coasts. There is, of course, great pleasure in reading of distant seas that one may some day sail (if one is young) or can never sail (if one is old), but I do not think I am alone in finding that the sailing books I take most often from their shelves are those that mention the sands, the headlands, the lightships and perhaps the very buoys with which in my own small vessels I have been familiar. "The buoys that were buoys when I was a boy," with which I have been on terms, almost, of Christian names, are the buoys of which I like to read. Further, granted that we do not move far in space, it is a great pleasure to slip backwards in time while looking at familiar seamarks. Today our coastal waters are bare of all sailing-craft but our own and a few—alas, every year fewer—spritsail barges. Middleton, in 1869, apart from steamships (of which he spoke with as much hatred as Mc-Mullen) counted " seventy-one ships in Flamborough Roads." Off Deal he saw " a large fleet of merchantmen spread over some two or three miles," and in the London River when he set out on his cruise " Large numbers of vessels, taking advantage of the strong breeze, were pressing down under square sails." Today the sight of one big sailing vessel is a memory to be treasured for ever. All the more delightful, therefore, to go back to share with Middleton the crowded coastal waters of the 'sixties, where the amateur sailor, working his little craft, is continually able to observe the professionals dependent as himself on making the best use of wind and tide. There is all this; there is the interest of the actual voyage and there is the interest of that extraordinary character, Middleton himself.

.   .   .   .   .

"Without a happy and suitable eccentricity of the person," wrote Empson Edward Middleton, " Greatness dwindles into Bigness." He was never in danger of such dwindling. There can seldom have been a man less inclined to conformity, even in early youth. At the time when he cruised round England and wrote *The Cruise of The Kate* his eccentricity was growing, though it was still no more than " happy and suitable." After all, there are those who think that all men are mad who go to sea when they could stay ashore, and that the maddest are those who, for pleasure, sail in boats of five tons and under, content with sitting headroom in the cabin and crawling headroom elsewhere. This is an arguable matter, with Dr. Johnson on one side and all small-boat sailors on the other. But even the small-boat sailors will agree that those of them who of choice sail single-handed are seldom ordinary men. They are of noticeably different texture, men of oak, not pliable. Their faith is in themselves, not in others. Their views are always their own. They do not search for precedents, but make them. They are, in the best sense of the word, originals. There are no doubters among them. Whatever they do is best done the way they do it, and though all the world be of a different opinion, the world is wrong for they are right.

Middleton's birth, circumstances and upbringing were such as to leave untarnished any natural eccentricity he might have. He was born in 1838, the son of Boswell Middleton, Advocate-General in Jamaica, who died of cholera when Empson Edward Middleton was fifteen. His paternal grandfather was Empson Middleton of Ebberston Hall, Yorkshire, who sank a large fortune in hunting for a coalmine and owned a documentary family tree that suggested that a title in abeyance was his by right. His maternal grandfather was Captain John Bradford, a Master of Trinity House, who "was held in high personal esteem by His Majesty King William the 4th . . .

and was very well received at Court." From him, no doubt, says the master of *The Kate* "I inherited the highly bred courtier-like address of my youth. . . . Even my children inherit courtier-like manners . . . and I have found them at 2 years old, walking backwards out of the room, bowing and scraping in the most approved manner, and entirely *on their own spontaneity*, without the faintest instruction from either parent." There were ship-owners on both sides of the family. His paternal grandfather had married a Miss Tindal of Scarborough, and when the Advocate-General died, his relations— "utterly incapable of understanding my naturally highly bred proclivities and regardless of the fact that I was likely to have considerable means of my own"—lost no time in bundling young Master Middleton off to sea in one of the Tindal ships, courtier-like manners notwithstanding, possibly in the hope of curing him.

Thus, at the age of fifteen, he sailed to Australia in the ship *Albemarle*, returning by way of India. Would-be officers in the Tindal ships had to do everything that was done by the able seamen, "so we learnt an extraordinary amount of seamanship in even one voyage, which lasted from a year and a half to two years." As a boy in the *Albemarle* he showed the remarkable gifts as a steersman which he retained in later life. The men, when engaged in difficult work aloft, used to ask for "the boy Middleton" to be sent to the wheel. Always, when steering a yacht, he refused to use tiller lines, which, he thought, caused each movement to be just too late. "You want to know as it were by instinct what the vessel *is going to do* and be just too quick for her, and yet almost imperceptibly fine." Admirably put, but there is more than a hint of eccentricity in his explanation. "When I happen to be fit and quite strong, I have a great store of electricity, such that either wheel or tiller will become charged, and that helps me to control it." Similarly, "I cannot mount a horse without its finding out that it carries an electrical person, and I do not require spurs." He did not dislike his voyage in the *Albemarle* and he "liked the ship amazingly," but "for all that my instincts told me that the mercantile marine was not exactly suited to me as a profession."

INTRODUCTION

"Had I remained, there is no doubt, I might have commanded a vessel at 25 . . . but what then, *the horror of steam set in,* and probably I would have been pushed aside, with all my seamanship and splendid caution, . . . and some *mere passed bookworm,* learned in engines, would have been foisted over my head." Writing in 1888, he said he thought he had profited by this voyage because it had led him at a very early date to question any motion of the earth and to disbelieve in its rotundity.

After his voyage in the *Albemarle* and his decision that the Mercantile Marine did not offer him a suitable career, he turned to the Army, only to be disappointed in his treatment by the Paymasters, details of which he somewhat irrelevantly set forth in *The Cruise of The Kate.* After some years in India he was sent home in charge of troops and, like some other young officers, took the opportunity of selling out and bringing his army career to an end.* He brought back with him the memory of some extraordinary exploits, such as his triumph over an Indian in a walking race of thirty-three miles, and an astonishing jump on horseback, some additional data to support his suspicion that the earth was flat, or, if not flat, most certainly not round, and an interest in military affairs that he never lost. Some of his notions, that must have seemed fantastic at that time, read today like intelligent anticipations of the forts of the last war built far out at sea for the defence of our coasts and (see pages 61 and 65) the Mulberry Harbours that were used in the invasion of Normandy.

After abandoning the Army as another unsuitable and for him unnecessary profession ("Being a gentleman, a profession could only lower my tone and narrow me up"), he presently set himself "to lift Poetry out of its then state of degradation" by means of a new translation of the *Æneid* of Virgil. He had, he thought, "the needful patience, and the bull-dog tenacity which is required in order to keep on rejecting everything but the best, and thus get at the truly artistic." He threw himself into the task of putting the *Æneid* into rhymed English penta-

---

* Ensign in the 51st Foot, March 30, 1858. Lieutenant, February 8, 1861. Retired by sale between March 1864 and March 1865.

meters with such ferocious energy as almost to bring about a breakdown in his health. He was suffering from insomnia and had overstrained his eyesight, when he picked up Mac-Gregor's *The Voyage Alone in the Yawl Rob Roy* in a Southampton bookshop. MacGregor was already famous. He had founded what became The Royal Canoe Club of which the Prince of Wales had agreed to become Commodore. Young men were following his example everywhere, and paddling their canoes on English and foreign rivers. Men listened to MacGregor no matter on what subject he was speaking. Shoeblacks, Ragged Schools, Training-ships for Boys, Protestantism, Canoes, MacGregor crusaded for them all, and with success. Middleton, reading *The Voyage Alone*, which tells how in his little yawl MacGregor voyaged from London to the Paris Exhibition, distributing tracts, organising a Canoe Regatta, and sailing back across the Channel, instantly decided that he would go one better, and be the first to sail round England single-handed. "My route gave me no difficulty; for I immediately determined to sail around England, choosing that course as the most difficult one I could think of, on account of its powerful tides." It was probably due to MacGregor's example that *The Kate* carried a cargo of printed matter for free distribution, but Middleton distributed not Protestant tracts but *The World of Wonders*, and hoped to acquire influence by his exploit so as to be able to persuade publishers to print his favourite book, Aristotle's *Ethics*, "in large print, for the poor to read."

When he sailed from London River Middleton had no intention of publishing a book about his voyage. He was concerned with the exploit, not with a chronicle of it. Indeed the voyage was to be an escape from literary work. The unforeseen result was *The Cruise of The Kate*, which, directly or indirectly, since the day when it "completely fascinated" Sir Arthur Underhill, has been an inspiration to succeeding generations of small-boat sailors. The writing of the book was "scamped," as its author freely admitted, and no one would read it for its style. Eighteen years after its first publication he revised it and produced a second edition, filling in here and there details that he had carelessly omitted when he first wrote. But by that time his eccentricity had grown and he filled his book out to much greater length with every kind of irrelevance. In the present edition the original text has been revised yet again. Those of his additions that are concerned with the voyage and clarify the story are here included, whereas those that have nothing to do with the voyage have been left out. Other omissions are a set of lamentable facetious verses on some Irish girls who visited *The Kate* in his absence, a rhapsody in prose and verse on an Indian landscape, and some reflections on the future of war which unforgivably interrupt his narrative as it moves towards its end. The resulting book gives exclusively in Middleton's own words a more intelligible account of the voyage than was given in either of the earlier editions.

.   .   .   .   .

It was a remarkable voyage, this cruise round England in 1869, not less but more remarkable because *The Kate* was accustomed to seek harbour for the night and made but few prolonged passages that she could avoid. Remember Mc-Mullen: "In the majority of cases where fishing boats are lost, they are swallowed up near the shore, and often at the harbour's mouth . . . there is more safety (in bad weather) in keeping the deep water and in not attempting to approach the land at all: where, owing to shallow water or currents, the sea will generally be found more dangerous." Apart from the more dangerous character of inshore seas, it is very seldom that water strikes a blow comparable in its effects with the slightest unintentional contact between boat and land, whether that land be stone, sand or wooden jetty. The ocean racers, far from courting danger, make a point of getting away from it and limit their acquaintance with the worst of it to those moments when they are leaving or returning to the coast. I think most people will agree that an "ocean race" is by no means so rigorous a test of seamanship as was for example Mr. Herbert Hanson's cruise round Ireland in 1933, when he took *Ianthe II* "inside everything with the exception of Eagle and Girvan Islands, where the swell rendered it inadvisable," or this cruise of *The Kate* when, in a very uncomfortable small boat, Middleton did his utmost to sleep and feed ashore and therefore was, day in, day out, close to the land with all its rocks, sands, tide-races and treacherous shallows. Not a single competent seaman but will admit that it is not on a passage in open water that he dare not leave the deck but before he is clear of the coast and after he has made his landfall.

It would have been a remarkable voyage if it had been carried out by no matter how experienced a yachtsman. But Middleton was nothing of the sort. Though he had been boy and seaman in a square-rigger, he had done no cruising in small craft, and had never been in sole charge of a boat until he set out to sail round England. His only preparation had been to hire a small cutter and a hand and to take a few lessons in Southampton Water. During these experiments he had never gone so far as to Calshot Spit, and the Light Vessel, when he saw it during his actual cruise, was to him "a new discovery." "Mooring and bringing up generally, were things of which I may say I knew next to nothing in connection with strange places." His practice sails had all been in the day-time and, in his hurry to be off, it had not occurred to him that he would need navigation lights. He soon found how necessary they were, and had a pair made and sent to Southampton, where he picked them up after doing without lights all the way from the Thames. Even then he had not considered the need of boards to carry the lights and to keep them showing as they should. Instead, he hung them in the rigging, and, as the lee-shrouds slackened, the red and green lights revolved and swung, an infuriating puzzle to vessels unfortunate enough to sight them. The first single-handed circumnavigation of England was the work of a novice, and of one who in writing his account of it was still not always conscious that he was telling a cautionary tale.

His was a difficult feat, much more difficult in 1869 than it would be today. Today it is nearly a hundred years since McMullen took the *Leo* " down Channel," and a hundred years of experience gathered by men sailing small boats have been made available to their successors in the files of the yachting magazines, and in such works as Cowper's *Sailing Tours*, Hanson's *Cruising Association Handbook*, and in books of detailed sailing instructions for special areas, such as Coles's *Creeks and Harbours of the Solent*, Messum's *East Coast Rivers* and Irving's *Rivers and Creeks of the Thames Estuary*. When Middleton set out in *The Kate* he had none of these things to help him. He had the Pilot Books that in those days took account of the needs of sailing coasters (which were, of course, much more useful to him than would have been the inferior modern Pilot Books which are meant for larger vessels proceeding under power) but, good as they were, they had not considered the needs of a very small boat dodging along the coast and seeking wherever possible to spend the night at anchor. McMullen would have suggested that he would find it easier and safer to keep away from the land, instead of deliberately keeping in touch with the shore, as he had set out to do, but in any case McMullen's first edition was not published until 1869, and in 1869 Middleton was afloat in *The Kate* and eagerly finding things out for himself. "To have known my way," he wrote, looking back on his youth, "would have been quite disgusting."

An auxiliary engine, no matter how sparingly used, would have made such a voyage comparatively easy. Middleton, with no engine, forced himself, in order to make the best use of his tides, to astonishing feats of indomitable rowing. "A real sailor," he says, "should always be fond of the oar, and should not seek to shirk the hard work of it, and the sometimes distressing hard work of it." "The man who has to anchor for tides, from want of energy to drive the boat over them, will never succeed in getting round England, unless, indeed, in a most favourable season." Read his summarised itinerary and see how resolutely he kept moving. Again and again he had to do with no more than two hours' sleep out of the twenty-four. Day after day he would set sail at whatever hour the tide served, and was prepared, in order to reach a harbour-mouth, or to round a headland before a change of tide should make it impossible, to row himself to utter exhaustion and to feel his pulse hammering in his brain-pan. Long afterwards he lamented that he had not written in greater detail of the physical efforts needed. Many a man who does not normally feel for engines the affection that is felt for them by some will, reading *The Cruise of The Kate*, be ashamed not to be grateful for that small team of willing horses stabled under his cockpit floor.

That he used pilots to take him into strange ports is not, I think, to be held against him. His business was to take his vessel from harbour-mouth to harbour-mouth. He needed the pilots not so much to show him the way in as to tell him where to put *The Kate* when once inside. Berthing was outside the terms of the private wager he had made with himself. "Nature," he says, "speaks very certainly to some men; but I am not aware that it will inform any man of a harbourmaster's rules." And again, "No man has a right to enter harbour by himself at the risk of damaging the property of others." Most of us have known moments in crowded harbours when we have wished that some other yachtsmen were as scrupulous. Once moored in harbour, having subsisted throughout the day on as little as a biscuit or two and a little sherry, Middleton would hurry ashore and, where possible, sleep and dine in a hotel. As the son of rich parents in the West Indies he had, no doubt, been waited on continually and had never acquired the elementary arts of looking after himself. His cooking arrangements aboard, though no worse than those that MacGregor and McMullen found adequate, were all but useless to him. He thought himself lucky not to have set *The Kate* afire, and, rather than wash and clean his own pots, pans, plates, knives, forks and spoons in the ordinary way, he did without anything but a pair of cups, a wooden salad fork shorn of one tine so that he could get it into his mouth, and a salad spoon that he also used for replacing his compass in its gimbals because the window in his binnacle was too small for his hand. His West Indian childhood may explain the indignation with which he learned that the washerwomen of Newquay would not do his washing for him on a Sunday, and perhaps also his belief that his status as a gentleman should have been enough to compel landladies and landlords round the coast to honour his cheques on sight. He forgot perhaps that in England "fine buccra gentlemen"

INTRODUCTION

are not distinguished by their colour from ordinary folk. Again and again he was faced by a demand for cash payment for food and bed, and on these occasions, even when he had money in his pocket and could pay, he refused and became so eloquent that north-country innkeepers accepted his cheques, or allowed him to leave without paying, when, if there had been any unpleasantness on the subject, he would, from some other port, send them the money he owed them in the form of postage stamps.

    •   •   •   •   •

The arrival of *The Kate* in the Thames after her voyage round England marked the zenith of Middleton's career. He had set himself to outdo MacGregor and he had in fact outdone him but, whereas MacGregor had only to show himself to find an audience the more eccentric Middleton was at first astonished, then angry, to find that to have sailed round England single-handed did not at once bring him the influence he felt he had earned. He wrote *The Cruise of The Kate*, thereby joining MacGregor and McMullen (the greatest of the three) at the very source of that stream of delightful books on sailing in small craft that has been steadily widening ever since. The eminent Longmans published in the same year both *The Kate* and the translation of the first two books of the *Æneid* on which Middleton's more serious hopes were set . . . but the walls of Jericho did not fall down. Undergraduates, delighted by the feats of the oarsman and sailor, were not at all interested in a translation of Virgil with whose hexameters they felt they had finished when they left their private schools. Middleton had expected an immediate success. Instead, everything went wrong. The "high art preface" he had written for his Virgil "was most improperly rejected by the publisher." The printer "studiously studied to destroy with commas" the "high art cadences" on which he had spent such pains. Disappointment must have hastened the development of an eccentricity that had been no more than "happy and suitable" into one that was neither suitable nor happy, but came at last to obscure even for well-wishers Middleton's remarkable gifts. In the second edition of *The Cruise of The Kate*, published from its author's private address eighteen years after the first, there are melancholy advertisements of his books, many of them, alas, unprinted but to be obtained directly from the author by subscribers ("Cheques to be made payable to Lieutenant Middleton, and will be filed but not presented until the work is put in hand"). They include a number of works on the measurement of racing yachts, on which subject he had a feud with the Yacht Racing Association. "My very income," he says "was crippled and penalised and this has arisen simply on account of the opposition raised by the Y.R.A. to the sale of my three books on Yacht Measurement, copies of which books were submitted to the committee . . . and some distributed to Royal Yacht Clubs." He also offered *The Author's Ledger*, on the best hand-made paper at nine shillings a copy, "showing an Author how to keep the account of his publications in the most concise and neat manner possible." He was now more than ever convinced that the earth was stationary and the sun moving and, further, that the sun was " but a very moderate remove from the surface of the Earth whose yearly harvests it has to ripen." Well, McMullen thought it likely that Heaven was in the sun, which he held was not so hot as generally supposed, and Columbus had believed that the earth was pear-shaped. Middleton offered ("if I can find 50 subscribers at nine guineas each" . . . "Cheques will not be presented until the work is arranged for with the printers") *The Stationary Earth*, "a reprint of all the Author's Letters and Controversies in Newspapers, with special high-class works issued from time to time containing precise Explanations of the Author's Diagrams on the Height of the Sun—with an exposure of the audacious folly of the Transit of Venus. . . ." "For the solution of this question I seem to be in a manner born—in that I am one of the rare instances of a person who has been professionally both Soldier and Sailor—and also very widely travelled." He devised "a feasible chart of the whole Earth," representing "a Basin Formation," "which bears out Genesis, Ecclesiastes, Job, David and Isaiah in a most remarkable manner." He made a furious onslaught on the Astronomer Royal, who treated his criticisms "with that defiant contempt which is the birthright

of at once the dishonest and ungodly in all walks of life."
There was almost no subject on which he was not prepared to
set his contemporaries right. He persuaded himself that a
pamphlet of his had inspired the policy of Disraeli and suggested that Indian troops should be based on Malta and other
islands and, "if carefully looked after with regard to comfort
and matrimony might be the means of supplying us with an
hereditary army." Disappointed by the reception of his
Virgil, "finding poetry quite overlaid by meaningless com-
pilations, somewhat consoled me with prose—until I progressed beyond that again into mathematics and figures."
His proposals grew wilder and wilder, and so did his geography. At the time of the Russo-Turkish War he wanted to
take possession of the Caucasus and the Crimea, to build a fleet
on the Caspian and somehow to join Batoum with the Persian
Gulf. He began to think of himself as a prophet divinely inspired and, in advertising his *Impeachment of Modern Astronomy*,
solemnly quoted "sacred verses" presented to his mother "On
seeing Popsy Middleton (himself as a baby) asleep aboard the
Swift Packet, on her passage from Falmouth to Barbadoes."
The verses included a prayer that the infant should

> . . . shine through all the dreary storms of life
> A splendid beacon in the world of strife.

He wrote, "I regard these verses with the greatest veneration
and reverence," remarked, "It is most singular that my life
has gravitated towards the prayer of these verses *without any
knowledge on my part of the said verses*," offered to sell photographs
of the original document at half a crown each, and announced
that such photographs had already been sent "to the leading
Societies and other Authorities in England." He must have
been a considerable nuisance and not one with which it was
easy to deal.

His quarrel with the Yacht Racing Association may explain
the curious fact that his name appears in Hunt's Yacht List
(which preceded Lloyd's Register of Yachts) for the year 1880
as that of the owner of *The Kate*, but does not appear in Hunt
for 1881 or subsequent years, though in 1888 he mentioned that

INTRODUCTION

he had designed and superintended the building of his own
"clipper yacht" and had taken out "several patents in yacht
construction." The 1880 entry shows *The Kate* as a 5-tonner,
25.5' over all and 7' in beam, built in 1869 and altered in
1874. In subsequent years, 1881 to 1886, *The Kate* appears in
the list without the name of any owner. She eventually "fell
into hands that did not understand her." Middleton must
have felt that her fate was not unlike his own, to be neglected
and misunderstood. His Virgil was ignored, the Y.R.A. continued to prefer their systems of measurement to his, and the
Astronomer Royal, utterly disregarding the proofs to the contrary offered by able critics who "in some cases have grown
grey as ruined men," held firmly to "the *unholy* and most
blasphemous and CREATOR-INSULTING doctrine of a round
globular world, rotating on an axis, and rushing forward
through space around the sun." Middleton sank into resentful
obscurity and his death in 1916 was almost unnoticed. No
matter; he had had his hour of glory and in *The Cruise of The
Kate* he remains after more than eighty years most obstinately
alive. It is impossible to read that book without being conscious of the almost physical presence of its author, eccentricities and all, and I hope that in this edition it will be enjoyed by
many who have never been fortunate enough to come upon one of
the rare surviving copies of the editions published in its author's
life-time.

THE CRUISE OF
THE KATE
1869

0   20   *Miles*   60   80

Greenock
Bowling
Grangemouth
Crinan Canal
Leith
Dunbar
Cockenzie
Irvine
Ayr
North Sunderland
Boulmer
Tynemouth
Hartlepool
Whitby
Scarborough
Filey
Bridlington
Donaghadee
Ardglass
Grimsby
Skerries
Howth
Kingstown
Wainfleet
Wicklow
Yarmouth
Lowestoft
Southwold
Courtown
Orford
Harwich
Milford
Skomer
Dale
Ramsgate
Lundy
Folkestone
Rye
Lyme Regis
Bridport
Southampton
Hastings
Eastbourne
Calshot
Boscastle
Hurst
Brighton
Padstow
Weymouth
Littlehampton
Newquay
Swanage
Selsey Bill
Plymouth
Torquay
Portland Bill
St. Ives
Dartmouth
Sennen
Cove
Salcombe
Falmouth
Penzance
Coverack

DESCRIPTION OF "THE KATE"

The Kate yacht is a small boat, twenty-one feet in length along the keel, twenty-three feet along the deck, and seven feet in beam. It has an iron keel, weighing over six hundred weight and an iron keelson of four, together with eleven hundred weight of ballast, cast in iron to fit the partitions built on the bottom on purpose to receive it. Its draught of water is three feet nine at the stern, and about one foot ten at the bow. The model is what a sailor terms "round"; that is, there is nothing cut away, as in boats built for racing purposes, which must sail fast in light airs, however bad sea-boats they may be. The model is so perfect that the water is felt everywhere, and the boat must rise gracefully and especially rapidly in a seaway; its quickness in mounting a sea is very remarkable, and that without any violent motion. The hoist of the mainsail, from the tack to the jaws, is thirteen feet; from the deck, about fourteen feet six inches. The hoist of the peak is just the total height of the mast, about twenty feet. The length of the mainboom is eleven feet six inches. The sail has three reefs and a balance-reef; each reef was ordered two feet six inches, but I believe there is a slight difference, the first reef being only two feet, as also in the jib, which was decidedly a large sail, being the full hoist of the mainsail and six feet on the foot. The mizen is also a large sail, and is, in fact, the least thing too large; it had one reef, about two feet deep, which was very frequently used. The storm-mizen was never set; it was too small for any practical purpose, but might have been useful in a very violent hurricane. The masts and spars were all made of Oregon pine, and looked very handsome when scraped. The bowsprit was a hollow, bad spar, and is a proof of how long a spar will stand if well stayed. It was very severely tested in many ways, but especially by the sea breaking heavily into the jib when beating to windward. I have often been astonished that it still remained when the deluge of water had passed; a deluge which was often several inches deep over the whole forward part of the boat, completely hiding it from view, and which would have drowned an open boat. The anchors were self-stocking, and very handy, but very unsafe. The stock was retained in its place by a notch, which worked through a slot in the head of the anchor. I had seen the necessity for and had ordered a couple of spring pins, to slip in through and prevent the stock turning round when the boat was going about at her anchor. The pins were forgotten. The iron worked as I had expected, and I have hauled up both anchors unstocked; after which I always slipped in a plug of wood, but that would work out, so that I cannot recommend the anchors without the *vertical* spring pin. The pictures of *The Kate* have created considerable astonishment to some of my friends. One bold horsewoman said she would rather her horse stood on one hair of his tail than venture in *The Kate*. Such being the case, I simply state that, where daylight allowed an opinion, the engravings have been toned down below the actual fact.

April, 1870.

CHAPTER I

THE START

MY wearied thoughts were wandering down the High Street of Southampton, during the Christmas week of 1868, and conducted tired limbs to the excellent circulating library of Messrs. Gutch, where faded eyesight fell upon a work bearing the title of *The Voyage Alone in the Yawl Rob Roy*. An instant sympathy with its contents created an exchange of matter; five shillings causing a deficiency of ballast in one pocket, while extracted essence of old clothes created a bulge in my starboard coat, correcting my proper trim, and allowing me to cruise to my usual station without more rolling than was actually necessary, in proportion to the paved or muddied depressions on the way. All hail *The Voyage Alone*. I am afraid to say how many times I read Mr. MacGregor's yawl voyage; certainly I have never met with any book of its class which pleased me so much. I read, then wrote to Messrs. Forrestt, of Limehouse, the builders of the *Rob Roy*, requesting all information about the craft; the correspondence ending by my sending an order for a similar boat with one or two slight alterations, such as a heavier iron keel, &c., to be ready on the 15th May. My route gave me no difficulty; for I immediately determined to sail around England, choosing that course as the most difficult one I could think of, on account of its powerful tides.

I may say I knew very little about sailing-boats at the time of writing the order for one, as I had passed several years, from 1858 to 1864, in the Punjaub, serving with her Majesty's 51st Light Infantry. I was fond of sailing when a lad, and went out sometimes in a small cutter, when residing at Jersey, but the oar usually offered the chief attraction: I presume from the fact that no one could meddle with my oar; whereas amateur sailing-boats, from stern to tiller, are rarely commanded by anyone. Tom seizing the tiller as often as not, without the slightest notion of steering; Jack the main-sheet, which would be much better belayed; the fore-sheet, the one which requires watching, being usually made fast.

The ocean was no novelty, for when fifteen years of age I went a voyage to Australia in the ship *Albemarle*. My respected father, the late Boswell Middleton, Esq., Barrister-at-Law, and Advocate-General of Jamaica, had applied for a commission in the navy, but the Government refused it because I was a month or so over fourteen, which, I believe, was the standard age for admission at that time. The merchant service taught me a great deal of seamanship, but especially how to steer under all difficulties. I liked the voyage on the whole, but came to the conclusion that the mercantile marine was not exactly suited to me as a profession; I therefore obtained a quittance from my cousin Mr. Tindal, the owner of the *Albemarle*, and bade good-bye to the sea as a profession. The army was not my choice, but the excitement caused by the Indian Mutiny led me to don the red coat, though the treatment I received very soon disgusted me with that service. The case was as follows. An officer sold out of the regiment in India on November 9, 1859, and appeared as gazetted out in the Indian papers. I was the senior ensign for purchase; my money was lodged, my examination passed; month after month went by without my name appearing in the *English Gazette*, and on the colonel writing to enquire the cause of delay, the answer received was that my examination papers had not arrived in England, and that I could not be gazetted until they were received. Such was the answer returned, in spite of the official announcement from the regiment and the colonel's assurance that I had passed the necessary examination. I was actually gazetted a lieutenant in March 1861. But how about the pay from November 1859 to March 1861? Doubtless you imagine my commission was antedated, and the amount, exceeding one hundred pounds, placed to my credit with the regimental paymaster? Not a bit of it; the whole sum was handed to the man who had left the regiment and virtually the service. So much for justice in the army! I sold out on the first opportunity, and am glad I did so, for my very blood would congeal if compelled to serve on such terms. Comparing the service with other professions, I think that the officers are disgracefully paid. It is no light thing to be an officer in the army; the duty banishes a man from his country. Not only so, but keeps perpetually banishing him. If he is in India, and has dared to make himself comfortable in one station, he is banished to another, from that to a third, and so on through a period of usually ten years; when, with good luck, he may find himself back in England, to be again rooted up at the end of three years and packed off to some new part of the world. Double their present pay could not even compensate for the utter loss of comfort and ties which usually make life bearable.

The next thing to be done after ordering the yawl for a single-handed cruise was to learn something about the handling of a sailing-boat. I therefore went out some dozen times during the winter months in a boat I hired from Mr. Stockham, a boat-builder in Southampton, and the boat-builder who has turned out the fastest and stiffest boat of its class in that part of the world. I failed to discover a yawl, but practised in a small cutter seventeen feet long, accompanied by a lad. The winter of 1868 was very severe, so that we usually started under reefed canvas. I often wondered how I should feel by myself, which puzzle I determined should be solved on board *The Kate.*

The amount of canvas to be carried was a most important question. The practice-boat had a seventeen-foot mainsail with reefs three feet apart. I noticed that when double reefed in a breeze she had hardly enough sail, but the single reef was too much. Five from seventeen leaves twelve, which was about what the boat could bear in a strong breeze. *The Kate* I knew would be a much stiffer boat, and so I determined the hoist of the mainsail should be thirteen feet, which, with a jib of the same hoist and a large mizen, would be as much sail as could be carried in a fresh breeze; and I have often had cause to congratulate myself that I had no more. The boat required a very great deal more in light airs, especially aloft; as my flag would sometimes blow out strongly when the sails were nearly becalmed. I can say nothing of the sailing of the boat in light airs—for instance, a two-pound breeze—for then a mainsail of twenty feet hoist, cutter-rigged over the stern, a long

3

jib-boom, with a powerful jib, converting the present one into a foresail, is about what the boat could carry. I imagine with that canvas it would be hard to beat, for when the breeze freshens, to suit the present amount of sail, it forges ahead at a great pace, and lies very close to the wind. A sea-way is necessary to bring out all the sailing qualities; the motion is then beautiful and easy, without any of the awkward plunging of sharp-built boats—in fact it is my belief that *The Kate* would drown most racing-boats of the day, especially when running either across a sea or dead before it. The model is so perfect, that seas have no chance of coming on board, for if they have any shoulder, the build feels it instantly, and rises like a cork. Seamen tell me that there are great curling seas which will swallow up anything; and I can fully understand that no vessel could live in the heavy breakers to be met with on the Cornish coast; but I have run before curling seas, of certainly from eighteen to twenty feet high, off Cromer, and yet nothing of any importance has ever come on board. I have looked behind and seen waves which threatened to curl right over me; but they always ran under the stern, the white water rushing along the decks on each side sufficient to drown an open boat, but of no consequence to a decked one. Again, the length of twenty-one feet is of the greatest advantage when running, for the boat only contends with one sea at a time; whereas the greater length is sometimes hung on two, and frequently overruns the seas. The wave usually carries *The Kate* along with it—for this reason, that the greatest beam is about three feet aft of the mainmast. The sea therefore holds on to that point and sweeps the boat along on its edge (if a curler) until broken, when the staunch little craft rushes through the white water as smoothly as possible. The lines were drawn by Mr. White of Cowes, and they reflect the greatest credit on the designer, for a more perfect sea-boat cannot float. If the same model was adopted by gentlemen who wish to possess a safe, handy sea-boat, we should hear of far fewer accidents, for it would take a very great deal to put *The Kate* over. My mast would not carry away; but then it is exceptionally thick, being nearly six inches in diameter. Four-and-a-half is quite enough, and I fancy would break before the boat could upset; that is, the power required to put the boat over would snap the mast. Such should be the proportion sought for when masting a boat; and for that very reason I should not advise unpractised amateurs to use wire rigging. I do not see how a boat can be upset when skilfully handled.

I take it accidents happen something after this fashion: a number of amateurs go for a sail by themselves, none of whom is fit to handle a boat, or has any real experience: no one in particular is told off to command, and if there should be, the rest would not obey. The breeze begins to freshen and becomes puffy; our amateurs all inwardly wish to have a reef down, but no one starts the idea, for fear of being thought nervous; consequently squall No. 1 half fills the boat, which squall No. 2 capsizes, and someone is drowned. Now, if a little real courage were shown by any one of the party insisting on a double reef and a hasty return to port, the sail would have had a satisfactory ending, and such an individual after a little chaff would have risen in the estimation of the rest. Real seamen are rarely caught, for they reef down before the breeze comes on. However, every one cannot be expected to have their experience; but a little caution may often take its place. I have frequently reefed down in the early part of my cruise, three or four times in the day, and that instantly I saw anything like a squall; and this practice of reefing gave me any amount of confidence in myself: I felt I could do anything I liked with the boat. Later on I often saved the trouble of reefing, when sailing through a mass of squalls off the land, by lowering the halliards a few inches, slacking off the tack, and making active use of the tricing-line. A good steersman can sail half the wind out of his canvas, and still have all that the boat can bear, in really dangerous squalls; but, as a rule, there is nothing so distressing as to see a man continually shaking a boat, and I am convinced that a great deal of very unnecessary risk is incurred by yawing about to avoid seas. My own motto is, steer as straight as possible. I had the sea right abeam, and heavy, when I crossed from Milford to Wexford. I should say the seas were about twelve to fifteen feet high, perhaps as large as any I have ever seen to the east of the Start in the English Channel, but I could not have made a course had I perpetually run the boat to leeward to avoid them. I kept the boat as straight as it would go; though at times not able to steer closer than four points; that is two each way. I let the boat run on occasions when a powerful sea swept it off, calculating the time it stood on that particular course, and kept it about the same time on the more weatherly course when thrown the other way—never attempting to seesaw over the exact line.

When a beam sea is to be avoided, wait until it is nearly aboard, and then the slightest movement will clear it. A sea on the quarter is the hardest to deal with, because it has a tendency to counteract the force of the rudder; but if caught just as the stern rises to the first part of the swell, the boat, if travelling fast, will pay off in time, with but a slight deviation from the course. Not only so, but it must be remembered that as the sea runs, the hollow runs, and if the boat is steered straight, the sea may often be beaten. Whereas if the boat is run off when in the hollow of the sea, the course suffers considerably: more care is necessary with an open boat than with a decked one, for the sea will come in to leeward. Long boats, when running, should always carry a large canvas bag in the shape of a sugar-loaf, called a drogue, securely fastened by a rope to either the mizen-mast or a thwart; a check-line fastened to the peak of the bag allows it to trail behind unexpanded. When the check-line is let go, the bag will fill, and thus check the speed of the boat.

The builders were very much behind their time, so that it was not till June 10, 1869, that I was able to take the boat out of Messrs. Forrestt's yard for the purpose of having the compass adjusted by Messrs. Lilly of London Street. The stores were all shipped on the 9th, but many little things required fitting, so that I dropped down to Greenhithe on the afternoon of the 10th with a couple of carpenters on board, and a hand to assist in swinging the boat, and act as pilot. I had never seen a vessel swung, so that I left the directions to others, who proceeded to moor the boat by lines on each quarter, the bow being held by the anchor, with the chain up and down. Common sense told me that the lines were not in their proper places; but as the men seemed to prefer their way, we blundered on till at last my method was adopted, viz., to moor with a line on the quarter and another on the opposite bow. I had at first intended having lead ballast astern, but was advised not to incur the extra expense, as the iron would answer as well. The iron does *not* answer as well, for it has a very great effect on the compass—so much so in *The Kate* that the magnets failed to reduce the error to a working allowance, compelling me to take the deviation; and wonderfully well Mr. Lilly has done his work, for I have found his card exact.

On the evening of the 11th, with the purpose of scrubbing the mud off the boat's bottom, I attempted to place it on a local hard, composed, as I had been told, of firm sand; but the patch of sand was very small, and at low water I found I had only added more mud; I therefore hauled off again when the flood made, and started for Sheerness with the first of the ebb on Saturday morning. It was not advisable to wash the decks as long as the carpenters were at work, but the water was not spared whilst going down the river, when I speedily discovered that the main-hatch leaked to such an extent as would have been dangerous in a seaway; I therefore anchored at Gravesend, and returned to the builder's yard with the next flood. The leakage was caused by the warping of that piece of the main-hatch which overlapped the forward coaming of the main hatchway. An evil may exist, but its detection may be difficult. The way to find out an error, in almost any case, is to place the subject in such position as we wish it to excel in. I shut the main-hatch as close as possible, stood inside, and looked for daylight. I found I could place a sixpence between the hatch and its drop-piece, through an opening of nearly three feet in width. I had a fresh drop-piece made, the seam along the deck twice caulked (the last time at Kingstown), after which not even one drop found its way into the cabin through that particular point, although the forepart of the deck was often invisible from the amount of water on board. There was a very fresh breeze up the river, which headed us

7

for the last ten miles; but the boat worked very well. The river was excessively crowded: large numbers of vessels, taking advantage of the strong breeze, were pressing down under square sails, and steamers of every size and description were ploughing through the water with an utter disregard for small craft in the way. I was standing towards the north shore, at one of the bends in the river, when I saw an enormous steamer suddenly come round the corner under full pressure of steam, and steering very close to the bank. It paid not the slightest regard to my boat; to go about was a doubtful experiment, on account of the crowded state of the river and the proximity of the steamer, and the wisest course appeared to hold on until I was compelled to stay or run ashore. The boat came round, but I was obliged to hang in stays, with the foresheet to windward, while the monster, some three hundred feet long, dashed past with the whole length of side barely four feet from my bowsprit end. The same thing, but to a less dangerous degree, occurred with another steamer a little further on.

Can nothing be done to prevent the reckless racing of steamers down a densely crowded river like the Thames? I am aware that steamers require a certain amount of speed to enable them to answer the helm quickly in a tideway, but I am certain that the pace at which these vessels were being driven was far beyond what is necessary for the perfect command of the ship. I have sailed down the river Indus, between Attock and Mooltan, where the channels are very narrow, being often only twenty or thirty yards wide, where the turns are excessively sharp and the stream very strong. Full speed is an absolute necessity for such navigation, and a novel sight it is to see a steamer rattling through a bight, or round a corner, at twelve knots an hour, with only a foot or so between the bow and the bank; which is frequently struck stem on, the stream setting steering at defiance. Full speed can hardly be necessary on the Thames, although the steamers are very long, for the curves are comparatively large and the stream broad, with its greatest force spread over a wide expanse of water.

I anchored off "Duke's" shore at Limehouse, but the number of barges which are continually passing down ren-

8

dered that anchorage unadvisable for the small yacht, which was dropped down to the City Canal Dock, and taken up to the builder's yard in the morning. Mr. MacGregor, the owner of the *Rob Roy*, very kindly came down to Messrs. Forrestt's yard, and made several very necessary alterations in the working of the main-hatch, bowsprit, &c.

The main-hatch is a most important article on board of a one-handed boat, and deserves special notice. The great desideratum is that it shall slide well forward, and yet be firmly locked in that position, so that in a strong breeze in harbour it may be open without any fear of the wind blowing it away; also that a minimum of friction may enforce a minimum of labour in the act of sliding it backwards and forwards. Each of these essential points is attained by simply maintaining the coamings to the full height for the exact length of the hatch; the forward part being sloped down towards the deck, also to the exact length of the hatch, which, when forward, will lie at an angle to its former position, but firmly resting on the coaming at the lower end; and the bearing on the side will always be less than the length of the hatch.

Everything was in readiness to haul out into the river at tide time on the 15th of June. My pilot was engaged to the Nore; but I re-engaged him to Ramsgate at my sister's request. There was little or no water to float the boat out into the river, but mud abounded to such a depth as required the combined power of about thirty men to drag the little boat into the stream; giving me a very satisfactory test of the strength of my rope cable, and rendering it serviceable by a good stretching. Everything was in readiness for a start by 7 P.M. The wind had been strong and puffy throughout the day; but who could possibly give the weather a thought when possessed of a bran new boat, bran new sails, rigging, flags, and experience?

With full sail we moved sharply downstream and progressed with much comfort until we opened a broad reach of the river, some three miles below Limehouse, where a sudden squall flung the boat over, putting two or three planks of the deck well under water, on which the mainsail was reefed, and then the jib and mizen. The north-easter increased rapidly, compelling a second reef in the mainsail, under which canvas we made Greenhithe about 9.30 P.M. The mud in the anchorage is rather treacherous; the best places were all occupied by a number of yachts, ships, and small craft. We had to put up with a berth below everything else, and let go the anchor on what turned out to be indifferent holding-ground. We made everything snug for the night, and turned in, after a friendly pipe, to sleep soundly till the morning.

I jumped on deck about 5.30 A.M., and found the boat had dragged the anchor and was slowly going ashore. The breeze had increased during the night, and was little short of a hurricane when I awoke. To have dragged on the ground would not have injured the boat in the least, as it is very soft; but the disgrace of going ashore on the first anchorage was not to be tolerated, so I called the pilot, and we made sail under a close-reefed mainsail.

We had a dingy with us of just the length to stow in the cabin. We had put it overboard at night in order to have the cabin for our own use; consequently it was astern in the morning, and was towed, as I wished to see how the process answered.

The waves were rather sharp and very short off Sheerness, where a metallic ring caused me to look round and see the cockle-shell being rapidly left astern, the towing-ring having pulled right through the stem-band. The sheets were instantly hauled aft, when the little *Kate* held a capital wind, standing on as stiff as possible: in the hard puffs a little deck would disappear, but at that point the boat refused to yield. Many a hard squall since then has shown that it would require enormous power to heel it over farther than is requisite to dip two or three planks of the deck. The first attempt to pick up the dingy failed, because it offers little or nothing to hold on by —a fact I had forgotten—and did not sheer the yawl close enough to allow of its being secured by hand; but I caught it on the second attempt by the rowlock, when the tiny craft was put below, the sheets eased off, and away we went past the Nore Light shortly after 9 A.M.

The pilot kept out at first for the Princess Channel, but

eventually steered over the flats; but not before the distance
was very considerably lengthened. Margate was passed about
1 P.M. at low water, and at a distance of two or three miles.
The sea round the Foreland was heavy, caused by the strong
flood making up against the wind, which at that time was very
hard. *The Kate* flew along at a great pace, shooting the sea
off the deck on either side like a waterspout, the powerful jib
preventing the boat from being thrown in the wind.* The seas
were just on the quarter, consequently the mizen had to be
stowed, as that sail assists to turn the boat round. Only one
wave broke on board; in fact, only the crest of that, for the
boat was on top of it in a moment. The distance to Ramsgate
from the North Foreland lay over water as smooth as a lake,
being very much sheltered from the wind. So much is this
the case with a north-easter, that an inexperienced hand in
Ramsgate would hardly believe that it was blowing hard with
a heavy sea within the short distance of two miles. Ramsgate
Harbour was made at 2.30 P.M. I had not shaken out the
reefs after rounding the Foreland; but it should have been
done, and the mizen ought to have been set, for there was
great danger of running against the pier-head, from want of
canvas to work to windward with in the light air; however, a
stronger puff chanced at the right moment, enabling the boat
to stay under a double-reefed mainsail and jib.

We moored along the quay, *The Kate* creating a great sensation among the seamen, who were greatly astonished at its
having been round the Foreland under the then conditions.
That sea, however, bad as it was, could not compare for a
moment with what the boat went through crossing the Bristol
and Irish Channels, and when running before the curling seas
round Cromer.

The 17th was passed in pumping out and putting the gear
in thorough working order. My pilot was an excellent
practical seaman, and was not content until he saw every rope
placed in the one best spot, and every deficiency provided for,

* The pace to Ramsgate was nothing like what *The Kate* did on other
occasions; but the wind was very unsteady, violent squalls compelling the
reefs to be kept in.

in the best and readiest way. The rough passage had very soon showed the necessity of some water-tight protection round the mast-hole and down the chain-pipe. I plugged the crevice round the mast with oakum and grease, which look much neater than canvas, and answered very well; I also used a plug of oakum to keep the water from running down the chain-pipe, but a considerable quantity found its way down in spite of that precaution. I provided the craft with a hand-pump, but after the first month its services were quite ignored, the sponge answering all purposes, and even that was not necessary under ordinary circumstances. A few gallons would find their way down the pipe at the end of ten days, or a hard beat to windward, but as a rule the boat was dry enough.

A carpenter was discovered who made a neat job of the dingy's stem-band. A fresh breeze set in from the south about mid-day, which caused the boat to heave a little, and made it necessary to shift over to the other side of the harbour. The unfortunate carpenter was on board, fitting the hatch-bolts; he asked me suddenly, with a very pallid countenance, to put him ashore, the boat having been hauled a few yards from the quay. I knew the dingy could carry two, for I had it up at Surbiton for a few days' practice, and several times took " Joe" the ferryman on board, sitting on the stern myself, our joint weights being something like twenty-four stone, which the boat carried well enough. Weight, however, requires arrangement. I calculated the carpenter was lighter than Joe; I therefore told him to get in, and sit on the stern, as he could not use the paddles. However, on my getting in, either from the weight being in the wrong place, or because the carpenter was not quite steady, the dingy quietly turned over, and gave us both a good ducking; no danger being incurred, because we had not even pushed off from the yawl.

Mooring, and bringing up generally, were things of which I may say I knew nothing; but now that I have had a great deal of practical experience in entering harbours, I would certainly advise any single-handed stranger to secure the early assistance of a waterman, who will point out the essential— that is, where the boat may be safely moored or anchored; for in every harbour which boasts a master there are certain places told off for certain sorts of craft, with respect to the depth of water and the keeping open the regular fairways. As a rule, a stranger in a boat drawing less than three feet of water can enter pier harbours such as Rye or Littlehampton by himself, provided that the tide is with him, but in making the voyage round England he will often make a harbour, with both wind and tide against him, in which case he must either bring up outside the harbour or be towed in. To anchor off for the night is out of the question where there is no regular roadstead, sometimes from stress of weather, but chiefly from the danger of being run down by fishing-boats and other craft. A light must be carried when outside; but lights will often go out, especially candle-lights depending on a spring, which is stiffened by the sea air, candle-grease, or natural failing of some sort.

I have said a stranger can enter by himself, simply wishing to point out that the accomplishment is easy enough; but it should be rarely attempted, for an immediate difficulty is encountered—namely, how to stop the boat. To throw down an anchor in many harbours is to lose it, for it will foul any amount of moorings, and if the boat is rounded to, the tide will carry it on at the imminent risk of damaging other people's property, as well as injuring the incoming craft. The single hand should therefore consider his duty performed in having made his passage, and should procure the aid of a second hand on approaching a harbour, and pick him up where he can, outside or inside; not to act as pilot, pilotage being unnecessary, but to guard against injury either to his own boat or that of some one else; for there can be no skill shown where there is no certain knowledge. It is no argument against the above to say there can be no skill shown in sailing round a coast utterly unknown to the navigator; for in that case there is certain knowledge that certain courses will clear certain dangers. Again, nature speaks very certainly to some men; but I am not aware that it will inform any man of a harbour-master's rules.

CHAPTER II

FROM RAMSGATE TO SOUTHAMPTON

SOME people have a great objection to starting expeditions on a Friday. That day with me has been rather a lucky one than otherwise; at any rate, no dire calamity has happened to the compass, for instance, because it was adjusted on a Friday, the charming needle pointed as correctly on that day as on any other, and the weather has also been propitious. Certainly the Friday on which I started from Ramsgate Harbour was as fine as any sailor could wish for. I found myself, on June 18, at 5 A.M., in a novel position; namely, sailing alone in a boat by myself for the first time in my life. Wondering how I should feel, I lit a pipe to consider the matter; but somehow the matter never turned up, unless an increase of spirits could be considered as such.

I made a circular course to Deal, so as to cheat the tide; the pier was passed at 7 A.M., when I found myself in company of a large fleet of merchantmen, spread over some two or three miles. *The Kate* had run past the greater number by the time that the South Foreland was rounded, and took the lead off Folkestone, as the others were more or less forced into the stream. Low water compelled me to wait for three hours, until sufficient depth would allow the boat to enter and be moored. I stood off and on for some time, and was carried by the strong tide to leeward of the pier, having kept a good way out to avoid a reef to the east of the harbour. The paddle assisted *The Kate* to windward again, when I threw down the anchor by the pier until the tide served. The harbour is lined with numbers of chains which form the moorings of the steamers and a perfect crowd of fishing-smacks: it was lucky that I employed a waterman to take the boat in and moor it, or I should certainly have dented my mahogany.

The harbour might be very much improved; it should be run out along the reef of rocks, which would give it a fine entrance instead of its present narrow one. The pier is certainly a curiosity of engineering, as the stones are at a slant instead of being perpendicular.

The Kate was ploughing through the deep, on Saturday the 19th about 5 A.M., before a very light breeze for the first hour; although it had been blowing strongly when I commenced to make sail. Dungeness was passed at 10.30 A.M., after which I steered straight for Beachy Head. The weather was unsettled, and wore the appearance of a strong wind from the south, which made its salutation off Fairlight and caused me to put a reef in the mainsail; but it was soon shaken out again as the southerly air departed, and left me in a calm. A fresh breeze from the north-west gave me great hopes of rounding the Head; but it suddenly flew to the west, to my intense disgust, dissipating all ideas of Beachy Head, and causing me to run all the way back to Rye. The clouds banked up very heavily astern as I was repassing St. Leonards, giving the appearance of a heavy squall; I therefore double-reefed the mainsail, reefed and stowed the mizen.

It was growing late, so I prepared for a night out, and lit the binnacle so as to have it all ready. I then passed some twenty minutes watching for a chance to sight Dungeness Point, its exact bearings being a matter of importance, because if I failed to make Rye Harbour I might have been compelled to run to Dungeness west roads. I had great difficulty in finding Rye, for the entrance to the harbour is very small and indifferently marked. I discovered it eventually by following some fishing-boats, about a mile off. The *Pilot Book* says Rye Harbour requires a pilot; I therefore hoisted my flag, but it was so small that the pilot could not make it out, and I was obliged to attempt the entrance by myself. I passed a smack on the way, a sailor from which kindly offered a hint if I would lay to; consequently the fore-sheet was brought to the wind. My friend came on board, and showed me to the entrance, where he departed, after giving me that most important information as to where I should round to.

The tide runs five or six miles an hour through a very narrow channel, causing a fall of several feet at the entrance.

Nearly all harbours of this description have a shifting bar, the position of which is frequently altered by the tides: and if composed of shingle, by nearly every tide or shift of wind. The variation in depth over the bar takes place so rapidly, and the tides are so powerful, that even the pilots cannot always make sure of escaping the ground. To enter Rye is hard enough, but for a stranger to bring up in the right spot is perhaps more difficult still; the tide gives very little time to determine which are the pilots' houses, forming the usual mark for rounding to. I found the fleeting seconds rather short in my blissful state of ignorance as to the eccentricities of architecture, and therefore chucked down the anchor—of course, exactly where it had to be picked up again; a manœuvre performed by a smart young waterman named Richard Morris, who in the course of a few minutes came to the rescue, and moored the boat securely.

The day's work had been fatiguing, so that I was glad to rest on Sunday, the 20th, although a fine breeze from the north-east continued throughout the day. I lost nothing with respect to the wind, for on arriving at Eastbourne I heard that the north-easter had not favoured that place, but that light westerly winds and calms had prevailed. I made sail on Monday at tide time, about 7 A.M., the boat being towed out of the harbour by the waterman who walked along the quay, the wind though favourable being insufficient to enable *The Kate* to stem the current. A nice breeze led me within a few miles of Beachy Head, when it met me from the west, setting in very thick, wet, and squally. I worked to windward for three hours in a driving mist without once seeing the land anywhere. The wind had freshened to a strong breeze. I therefore double-reefed the mainsail. The mizen outhaul got loose, and blew out astern while I was reefing that sail, consequently I had to venture out on the boom and secure it before it unrove altogether. The boat-hook would have answered the purpose, but I did not think of it at the moment.

The danger of getting overboard is one which I can always afford to laugh at, as long as I have hands and feet to claw hold of something with. I slid down the starboard leach of

16

the main-topsail on board the ship *Albemarle*, whilst running before the wind, and have stowed the whole three royals when it was so dark that I well remember holding up my finger on the main-royal yard to try if I could see it; the lightning on that occasion being of the most vivid description.

The most unpleasant sails to handle in a ship, as in a boat, are those at the extremes, the mizen and the flying-jib. I have loosed the mizen on board the *Albemarle* when the peak was banging about from side to side, and on one occasion the sail was actually hauled out before I had time to get off the spar. Captain Stephens happened, luckily, to step on deck, and immediately ordered the sail to be brailed up, the guys hauled taut, and myself to descend. I will add for the information of the uninitiated that the mizen-peak has no foot-rope on it whatever; the flying-jib has, but it is usually proportioned to a man's height, is always more or less greasy, and at a very considerable slope. My jib and mizen have given me very considerable trouble to reef. I carry a shifting mizen and jib, but prefer to reef, because the storm-sails are thus kept dry and fit for use when they are wanted. Besides, they are too small to be set, except in a hurricane. I usually bring the fore-sheet to windward when reefing the jib, slack the halliards a little, and haul the earings down. The best way to deal with the mizen is to stow it, which is about the same thing as reefing the mainsail, and answers very well, as the boat works to windward under the mainsail and jib.

At the end of the three hours, a squall lifted some of the clouds off Bexhill, which appeared dead astern, bearing north-east. The tide had turned against me; I therefore ran back and brought up at Hastings, where I made arrangements to be hauled up on the beach if it came on a gale from the southward. At Hastings they have large standing windlasses, to which they can take capstan bars at any moment, and run larger and heavier vessels than mine on the beach very promptly, should the necessity arise. By 1 A.M., however, the falling tide would have uncovered the rocks, made those arrangements impossible and compelled me to look out for myself.

17

The sea between Dungeness and Beachy Head may be considered as one large bay; and looking at it in that light, my position in a southerly gale would have been much the same as that which a board of examiners are said to have pressed upon an unfortunate midshipman.

Question number one being: Your ship is embayed, sir; what will you do?

A. Beat her out, sir.

Q. She will not beat out?

A. Let go the anchor.

Q. The anchor drags?

A. Let go another.

Q. She still drags?

A. Club haul, sir (that is, drop a gun overboard).

Q. Still she goes astern.

A. Throw some more guns over.

Q. She breaks all her cables and drags in spite of everything.

A. Let her go ashore, and be d——d, sir.

I would have thrown the kedge over, with as much iron ballast attached to the cable as I could manage to fasten on, if caught in a like position. To do so neatly it would be necessary to attach a second line to the cable at such distance as not to foul the anchor, and fasten the ballast to that. With a view to this assistance in a heavy gale, where the anchor must hold, or the boat go ashore, each hundredweight of ballast should be cast with a rounded iron handle, so that each piece could be strung on to the spare line, and as much chafe as possible be avoided.

In the early morning I started again for Beachy Head with a light air north-east: but things took a contrary turn, and a most paltry air of wind set in right ahead. I had to turn to windward to Eastbourne, paddling nearly all the way. I passed that place at an offing of nearly two miles, at about half-tide, and stood on a long tack through the heavy overfalls, allowing the boat to race along, feeling certain of making Newhaven, if not Brighton. I was much astonished at seeing a young flood making up inshore, just opposite to

Cuck Mere Creek, and went about instantly so as to benefit by the remaining tide outside, still hoping to weather Seaford Cliff; but on the return tack *The Kate* dropped back to the coast-guard station. The truth was only too plain: my informants were utterly wrong about the tides. I had started under the impression that I should carry a long ebb when once round, because the tides divide off Beachy Head. The tides do not divide off the headland, but run east and west past Eastbourne with no half-tides, dividing between Hastings and Rye somewhere off Fairlight.

As I was standing in the last time I saw one of the coast-guard running along the cliff, evidently to warn me off, for when I put up my helm, he wore ship. There was far too much swell to think of bringing up in Berling Gap, especially as the wing was right on the land; *The Kate* had therefore to run back the six weary miles it had gained. I nearly struck on the reef which runs a considerable distance off the point, much farther than I had allowed for; consequently I was right upon the shoal, and had to dodge the rocks by hauling rapidly to the wind and then paying off again. I worked clear in that manner, but had to pass over many rocks which were thickly packed together. A small boat with an iron keel would not come to much harm even if it struck on the reef, for the rocks are flat.

A new difficulty presented itself off the northern point, and dodging had again to be resorted to in order to clear the sands, which uncover at very low tides. Large whirling eddies marked the most hazardous spots, where the water was thickly discoloured by the sands. I cast anchor eventually off the fort at Eastbourne, re-entering the social circle of humanity by enjoying a friendly chat with a waterman who came off to inspect the novel-looking craft. Strangely enough, he brought a baker with him, who supplied me with bread and biscuits, whilst the seaman gave me correct information about the tides, and departed, promising to come off and put the boat ashore if necessary.

It is often requisite to haul yachts and small craft on the beach both at Hastings and Eastbourne, and the needful apparatus is always ready, as also a number of greased boards to prevent the boats' bottoms from injury, the charge being the moderate sum of five shillings. I would not have run to Rye had I been aware of this fact, but would have brought up off Eastbourne on Saturday, and have rounded Beachy Head either on Sunday or Monday, with a clear gain of at least forty-eight hours.

I again attempted Beachy Head on the 23rd, on the top of the tide; and brought up off Brighton at 3 P.M. The appearance of the boat brought off many admirers, so that my society commenced as usual, and if it was not very entertaining, at any rate it was free from misconstructions.

The ebb made away at 11 P.M., but I determined to start at 1 A.M., so that I might have a short nap, and by being true to myself be able to be true to the boat. I found sleep out of the question, and commenced to set sail about 12.30 A.M. It takes a very considerable time for a single man to get under weigh, because every little thing has to be done by one hand; and if the chain anchor (weighing 56 pounds) is down instead of the 20-pound kedge, it is smart work to be under weigh in half an hour, with every rope in its proper place, and the dingy stowed inside. It is no joke to lift a large anchor in some of the best holding grounds, but I have never failed to get it. If there is a stiff breeze ahead, the single hand will find it much the best not to hoist the jib until the anchor is off the ground, for the boat is required to shiver in the wind, whereas if the jib is up, and either sheet made fast, it will head off at a sharp angle, making it almost impossible to get the cable. I have found it necessary to hoist the jib when the anchor has been brought up and down, but offered a great resistance in very stiff blue clay. On those occasions *The Kate* and I, pulling together, have always proved victorious.

I noticed, when passing Worthing, that its light was not visible, though the street lamps could be plainly seen. I mention the fact because it is of the utmost importance that the lights along the coast should be kept in proper order. I should say at a guess that I passed Worthing at a distance of two miles from the land, and saw all the other lights distinctly.

It was necessary to bring up at Little Hampton that the tide might flow to such depth as would allow of my crossing the rocks to Bognor. The best anchorage for small craft at dead low water is about one-third of a mile in front of the harbour mouth, in the slack water between the two tides on a sandy patch. The time to be passed in waiting for the tide offered a good opportunity for cooking breakfast; the plates were arranged, and I was in the act of emptying the tin of beef-steak, when I saw a coaster dash out of the harbour to-wards Bognor. To remain at anchor when it was possible to progress was not to be thought of, for on leaving Brighton I had determined that Southampton should be my next port, and that I would not cast anchor elsewhere, except as a tem-porary necessity to await the tide. The tin of beef was returned to the boiling pan, the two mouthfuls were hastily swallowed, the plates, &c., put away, the anchor tripped, and away went *The Kate* in full chase.

The vessel in front took the ground twice, thus giving me ample warning and making it an easy matter to overtake it, whereupon I received some excellent information as to the best course to keep with regard to the tide, and distributed some light literature, which was very thankfully accepted: the *World of Wonders* being everywhere considered a great boon by the seamen. The wind headed me and fell light when some five miles east of Bognor. I therefore commenced very early with the oar, and paddled all the way to Selsea Bill, rounding that point about 2 P.M. I made a very good course to Ports-mouth by the aid of my parallel rulers; but the weather was very hazy, and not knowing Hayling by sight, I mistook it for Southsea, and ran the boat off the wind, the entrance to Paignton * Harbour showing me my error.

A haul to windward placed me in a very unpleasant position, the boat being becalmed about three miles to the west of the south Spithead fort, and 1½ miles south of Hayling sands, when the flood tide began to make up. I had already paddled the equivalent of fifteen miles, had passed one sleepless night, and, with the exception of about two mouthfuls of steak, had eaten nothing but a piece of bread. To be carried back by the

* Paignton occurs in both editions, but must be a misprint for Langston.

tide was not to be thought of, at least not one inch further than I could help. The maintaining of this principle has had a great deal to say to the entire success of the expedition. When a man is exhausted let him throw down his anchor, but not before. In my particular case I was anxious to save twenty-fours into Southampton Water, for although the distance from Brighton is not much for a boat rigged for and handled by one man to travel in the time with even a slight wind, if fair; if foul the greater part of the way, it is a very good twenty-four hours' work. Be it understood that I can only work one oar at a time, and then if there is the slightest pressure on the canvas the boat will steer very well, if close hauled; but not so well if going free, or becalmed.

The Kate was carried back for the first half-hour, as I could see by the sands, but slight puffs of wind enabled me to make up the slight loss during the second, the tide all the time setting me towards the north shore. Rejoiced at holding my own, and feeling certain of ultimately beating the tide as I neared the shore, I stopped to drink a glass of sherry with an egg in it, and then set to work again, the boat's head being due west by my compass with south Spithead fort on the port bow, and a large man-of-war to starboard. The paddle never stopped for another hour, the fort being brought more to port, the man-of-war first ahead, and then also to port, the boat's head maintaining the same compass course; the sands had covered, but the seaweed showed me I was winning the day. At last the fort was made, about one mile ahead on the port beam; a very slight but steady air took much of the weight of the boat off my hands, and I began to gain fast, the tide having put me close into the north shore.

I had the fort abaft the beam at the end of three hours, and enjoyed the proud satisfaction of having won the hardest physical struggle of my existence. I am afraid I was just a little indiscreet at this point, for I instantly drank everybody's health in another glass of sherry. Things differ in this world: my glass was perhaps a little large, being composed of some peculiar metal which in the present day passes for silver, and held exactly half a pint.

I passed Portsmouth Harbour about 8 P.M., and might easily have ended my labours, but a lovely north-east breeze sprang up, and mindful of my determination of making Southampton, I held on in spite of the second night which threatened. I was continually nodding while passing Southsea and Monkton Fort, but always picked myself up just in time to save any dire calamity; twice the boat was all but on the shore, but instinct instantly aroused the nodding helmsman. It is wonderful how soon a man will become part of his boat, and will feel every move out of the proper course; in fact, a sudden turn is distinctly felt. The treacherous breeze carried me a mile or so past Monkton Fort, when calmness reigned around, the night setting in dark and cloudy.

The lights were very puzzling. The *Pilot Book* certainly gives all information, but it is too diffuse, and its general arrangement is bad, requiring the book itself to be studied before its eccentricities are discovered. This should not be. All the information on any one point should be noted under one head; and not scattered about the book, the course being on one page, the nature of a light on another, or left to be discovered on the chart. On looking at the *Channel Pilot Book* to discover the name of the revolving light on the north shore, I failed to make it out. I ascribed the want of instruction in my letter to the *Field* (written without reference to the *Pilot Book*) to my then fatigued state, but now that it lies open on the table I can refer the reader to pages 52 and 53, which profess to be a guide through the Solent, and which actually mention the light without stating its nature, leaving the mariner to hunt it on the chart (where it is marked as a revolving light), or to turn to page 95 for the necessary guidance. Important works such as pilot books should be written on a scientific principle, the writer always maintaining the same order of mention, and making a careful detail of the necessary points, such as the nature and number of lights; distinctly stating their colours, whether they are fixed or stationary, and their exact bearings with some other point when such can be given; tides, their force and direction, with points of division exactly stated, and not scattered in a hazy sort of way over twenty miles of headlands, as is the case with Beachy Head; the hour of high water on the days of full and change of the moon. Leading marks should not be So and So's house, for strangers will not know So and So's house, but there should be some prominent mark which can be recognised by everyone. If courses are laid down, let them be most carefully considered—and not, as in *Manse's Guide*, calculated to require a succession of heavy dews to float the ill-directed keel. Other works should be consulted with a view to their beginnings and endings. It seems almost incredible, but it is a fact, that two men have written pilot books, one for the English Channel, the other for the Bristol and Irish Channels; and that neither work makes mention of the north coast of Cornwall, there actually being several miles of coast, north and south of St. Ives, utterly neglected.

The book which I have found most serviceable is the *Pilot Book of the NE. Coast*, issued by the Admiralty: the cuts of part of coast, lighthouses, &c., are particularly useful. Even So and So's house might pass as a leading mark if accompanied by a picture of it. With respect to harbours, the direction of the entrance should be clearly stated, and instead of giving a course into the harbour, beginning goodness knows where, let a line be drawn through the exact centre between the piers or other entrance, showing the precise point to which the harbour faces. Harbour tides also require especial notice. A book or series of books giving the above information all classed in one and the same order, under one heading, and accompanied by correct charts, pictures of headlands, lights, houses, &c., would be invaluable to the coasting trade and yachtsmen.

I again put the paddle out when the breeze deserted me, and kept for the light on the north shore; the tide came with a rush about 11 P.M., and swept the boat rapidly along. I heard a large ship let go her anchor just ahead at 12.30 midnight, and as I passed I did the same, hailed the vessel, and heard the grateful news that I was in the Southampton Water, just off Calshot Castle. The ship had been floating close by *The Kate* for hours, but it carried no light, and the darkness had prevented my seeing it. A large ship will be carried by the tide almost as fast as I can paddle with it, without using extraordinary exertion. I threw down the heavy anchor, because I was afraid I might go to sleep. To avoid this, instead of putting the dingy overboard, and thus giving myself room for a good sleep, I merely squeezed myself in an upright sitting position into a corner of the cabin close by the dingy, a position which would allow of my dozing without actually falling into a sound sleep.

There is only about three hours' tide in the Southampton Water, and my anxiety not to miss it kept me constantly on deck peering into the utter darkness and watching the tide. I washed decks about 3 A.M., and tripped the anchor at 4.30 A.M., when the tide had slacked. Had I waited for the tide to turn, I should have been in an awkward position; for just ahead of *The Kate* another vessel was at anchor (which also had neglected to hoist a light). I was in ten fathom water, and before I could have stowed my anchor, the tide on the flood would have set me right across its bows. Such little matters are of vital importance to the single hand, but the danger of collision may nearly always be avoided by tripping anchor at the right time. A fresh north-east breeze carried me up the Southampton Water to the pier, where I cast anchor at 6 A.M.

The Kate was beaten by one vessel only on the way up, a very smart-looking coaster of some 300 tons, and that because it got into the centre of the tide, just a few minutes before I steered into it, having been obliged to hug the shore at first because of the ebb. I was amused at seeing the fishermen trying to beat me up the river, the only piece of water that I knew: they kept on the west shore, making tacks to keep in the young flood; I stood right across the ebb to the other shore, where I knew the water was deep enough for my craft, where I was to windward and in the young flood. They ran aground, I sailed on.

I was very much fatigued after being out for two days and nights without sleep or proper food: as for my hands, they were swollen to such an extent that for several days I could not shut them, each finger looking for all the world as if it had the dropsy. The rough ropes had made many open sores in

THE CRUISE OF THE KATE

addition, which required time to heal: I was therefore glad of a
few days' rest, and took the opportunity of revarnishing *The
Kate*. The seams had swollen and squeezed out the putty in a
succession of ridges, which had the effect of stopping the boat;
these had to be removed with pumice-stone, when a fresh coat
of varnish was laid on. The work had to be done between
tides, and the varnish had hardly a fair chance of drying before
the water made up, so that it turned the bottom a dull sort of
white. I have found that the best oak varnish will keep the
weed off very well, but a thick slime gets on which is almost as
bad. To remove it, I had the boat scrubbed, when the weed
grew, instantly, for the simple reason that the varnish was
scrubbed off. I found it necessary, as a rule, to scrub the
bottom once every ten days.

I was advised to get a covering for the well with a small
hole in it, and a curtain so that I might lash it round my body
when running in a heavy sea. No such thing is necessary, and,
what is more, no such thing can be used by a single hand, for
he must be at liberty to move rapidly, so as to work the gear.
Such a protection might assist in keeping your toes dry, but
nothing else, for when the sea is abeam, and the drift is flying
over the mast-head, the water will trickle down your neck, and
wet you through and through, even if you sit as close as wax.
If the jib-sheet can foul anything it will, especially when beating to windward through spoondrift, and a jump forward
must clear it: mine invariably made love to or quarrelled with
the jib reef earings, which, being jealous from want of attention, embraced the sheets, and jammed tight in the blocks.
However, jib reef earings are, I believe, rather out of date, so
that nuisance need not be suffered much longer. The anchors
remain, and if the slightest part works loose, the sheets will
take a round turn instantly, for when there is a breeze on, the
weather sheet must be let go with one hand, while the other
cannot command the lee one instantly. The sail therefore flies
out with such violence as sometimes to unreeve the weather
sheet, unless knotted as it should be; but in either case a jump
forward must follow unless the end is made fast. I always ease
the weather sheet over as much as possible before I let go; but

26

do what one can, in a hard breeze, with one hand, it is impossible to prevent the sail blowing out.

A peculiar dog-like watchfulness is very quickly generated by being entirely by oneself without even a dog to keep guard at night; and that faculty is always awake. The first notice I got of it was at Southampton, where I stayed three days, sleeping in my mother's house. I found myself, about 12 midnight, standing at the window, under the impression that I was running ashore. I put up my hands to dash the main-hatch off, so as to let go the anchor, for the darkness inside the room, and the brilliant moon outside, caused me to imagine I was peeping through the small aperture I always leave for ventilation by not pushing the hatch quite home. Discovering where I was did not startle me on that occasion, for the danger appeared a long way off, and I quietly went to bed again. However, the next time it happened was at the Imperial Hotel in Torquay, where, from the rocks being excessively defined and very close beneath the window, my heart on my awaking might have been heard beating a hundred yards off.

Later on I contracted a regular habit of going on deck when fast asleep, and yet perfectly alive to everything. I amused a man very much at Leith by one of my nocturnal looks around. I had been laying off the pier for thirty-six hours, and was going to start next morning. I was on deck about 12, as usual, with the impression which was always uppermost, that I had arrived at some new place. On seeing the man, I asked him where I was, and he said, "Well, sir, you ought to know by this time; you have been here long enough"; whereupon I gave a satisfied grunt or two, and turned in again. I wish it to be distinctly understood that on these occasions I was perfectly aware of everything that went on, and remembered everything when awake.

I got very acute after a time, and would reason the matter with myself. I remember saying to myself at Lowestoft (where I always slept on board for an early chance), "Now, I am not going to be taken in this time; there is the pier light, there is So and So"; on which I turned in quite satisfied. To such a pitch did this faculty of watchfulness arrive that I knew everything that went on, and morning after morning I have been extremely puzzled to make out if I had been asleep at all or not. Still, I was always quite fresh from any fatigue of the former day. A dog would doubtless have prevented any such peculiarity, and would have allowed me to sleep as sound as a top, except when disturbed by positive noise, which in truth was often enough.

The dingy was a great source of annoyance, for if lying astern, the slightest air blew it against the side, and awoke me by a most irritating succession of little bumps. I resorted to many dodges before I discovered the correct way to fasten the little one; and even then in a seaway the cure was nearly as bad as the disease. The best way to secure the dingy is to put three fenders over the side, close together, and then lash the boat's stem firmly against them with a forward and aft lashing; but as I have hinted, in a rough roadstead the motion of the dingy was so violent that the constant thud could be plainly heard, with every now and then a whack against the rail, which no manœuvring could prevent, as long as the cockle-shell was not hauled bodily on deck. Such would seem a final cure, and with regard to the dingy doubtless it was, but the rigging was as bad as *Cheemaun*;* tighten the gear as much as possible, in an hour's time, if there was a breeze, ruckle, ruckle, ruckle compelled attention to one rope, which had dried and consequently stretched; in another hour or so ruckle, ruckle, ruckle again demanded instant stoppage, and if the dingy was on deck it lumbered up the ropes so that they were got at with great difficulty. In fact, I never saw such a rebellious crew as they were between them.

* *Cheemaun* was the name of the dingy.

CHAPTER III

FROM SOUTHAMPTON TO DARTMOUTH

ON Tuesday, the 29th, I took leave of my darling sister (who had raced down from London on purpose to see me), said good-bye to my mother, escorted a lady cousin on board the Jersey packet-boat, and went to sleep on board the yawl, intending to start when afloat in the morning. I had engaged a man to wake me up, and lend a hand to get the boat afloat: and well it was I did so, for the tides were making off, and the water did not rise as high as on the day before. It required our joint efforts to push *The Kate* off: in fact, nothing but the *voûs* of my assistant would have prevailed. He was a man of action, and without hesitation produced a large lever, which he placed beneath the bows and heaved while I hauled on the stern rope; we hauled out inch by inch, until one good lift and haul floated us right away.

I had very little sleep during the night, but arose before my assistant came; and though I put many things in their proper places, I had to pick up a mooring when afloat, and spend at least half an hour in putting the gear ship-shape before I made sail for Weymouth. I was an hour and five minutes doing the six miles from Southampton pier to Calshot Castle, with a light breeze which fell off to next to nothing; the flood met me at 8 A.M., and I rounded Hurst Castle right in its teeth. The tide was boiling along by the "Needles," and it certainly appeared a risk to attempt to stem it with such a very light air. I kept as close as I could to Hurst, feeling the depth as I went along with the boat-hook, which is much handier than the lead, and had as much wind as I could carry round the point, although nearly becalmed on the weather side.

Every strong tide, as a rule, makes an eddy by the land, consequently, "O single hand," never be alarmed at strong tides. Like everything else they only require a little management: where they do not throw off an eddy and run six knots an hour they must be taken at the slack, if against. Such is the tide round Portland Bill, and if that passage is attempted at the wrong moment, even a gale of wind from a favourable quarter will not save the craft from a journey through the race; for the instant the bow touches the tide, it will whirl the boat round, throw her up in the wind, or dead before it; when a broken spar or two may add to the other little comforts in store. The eddies round Hurst Castle are very large and powerful, and appeared to set towards the tide-way; they are decidedly the worst I have been through.

After rounding Hurst I made for Christchurch Ledge buoy and thence took a straight course for Swanage, but owing to the deficiency of the chart, I was sorely puzzled to make out the headlands. The only charts I used for the south coast are those annexed to the *Pilot Book* above mentioned. The scale is small, and therefore allowance must be made, but I have found that many of the Admiralty sheets are not drawn out as well as they might be. If a thing is worth doing at all, it should be done as well as possible. The headlands are not sufficiently defined; but, worse than that, the bays are not properly indented, nor are the numberless neat little anchorages taken the slightest notice of. I presume the Admiralty sheets are expressly for the coasting trade; but to be really serviceable every little refuge should be carefully noted, each headland strictly defined, and each bay represented. The perfect success of everything in this world depends upon each minute detail being considered. Peveril Point is not marked in the chart I made use of, although it has a small but very hot race tide off it, which is mentioned in the work. There are several headlands between it and St. Alban's, none of which is noted.

I put into Swanage Bay to make enquiries, and as the wind headed me on going out again, I put *The Kate* through the race off Peveril Point, so as to save making a tack to windward. My informant in the bay had told me there was enough water over the rocks, and as I had no experience of what a race was like, I thought a little might be serviceable further on, if caught in the St. Alban's or Portland races. The one inevitable sea came on board, drenching me through and through. The sea in a race over rocks is perfectly furious, and rushes at the boat from all sides at once; but much of the commotion depends upon the state of the tide. A race over a sand—"furit æstus arenis"—usually takes the form of overfalls, creating great curling seas, which break heavily, and are always more or less dangerous, according to the depth of water on the banks and their distance apart. The shallower the water, the closer the waves and the heavier they break. I had been advised to keep close in to St. Alban's so as to escape the race; I did so, and was into it before I knew that I was off the head; the race, as a rule, runs right away from the rocks, leaving no passage for a sailing craft; though fishermen in small boats often pull in-side. I did not pass through much of the race, but from what I saw it appeared of a mild character. The whole way between St. Alban's Head and Portland is one huge race in bad weather, and dangerous to vessels of all sorts; but in fine weather, with the exception of that off Portland, there is not a single race on the south coast which an open boat may not pass through in perfect safety. They look far worse than they really are, as every danger does. I feel certain that most yachtsmen will agree with me in laughing at such races as those off the Land's End, Lizard, and Black Head. But the races off Lundy Island and the St. Goven's Bank in the Bristol Channel are highly dangerous in bad weather or even a stiff breeze. In the latter, especially, the seas are excessive without any wind at all: but vessels can then be kept in command, whereas in the Portland race it is a frequent occurrence that even steamers cannot be steered.

St. Alban's is an insignificant headland, marked by an in-significant lighthouse. The coast to Weymouth affords several snug little anchorages and is exposed to violent squalls off the land. They whistled down the gullies with great force on the day that I passed, making an active use of the tricing-line a constant necessity.

I entered the harbour of Weymouth between 8 and 9 P.M., and was on the point of throwing the anchor down, when a waterman informed me that if I wanted to lose it I was going the right way to work, as the bottom was a mass of moorings. I therefore surrendered *The Kate* to his guidance and was snugly moored for the night.

I started on July 1 at 10 A.M. to round Portland Bill, the worst point on the south coast of England. There was a nasty lop of a sea in the bay, but not much wind. The great object was to arrive at the point when the tide was slack, and in order to make certain of doing so I reefed throughout, to the great astonishment of some watermen, who took the trouble to inform me that it was not blowing. The position of the race is always a matter of doubt, for it shifts with the wind, being sometimes half a mile off the point, and at others right on it, or leaving a very narrow passage. It is usually to the east of the Bill during the flood and to the west on the ebb. All these complications render it the harder to escape being swept through, for if the vessel is before the time, the flood will set it through; and if after, the ebb will often do likewise. I made the point at slack water; but still met a tolerably strong tide, and had to shake out the reef, and paddle as hard as I could for at least thirty minutes, before I gained the few important yards and was able to put my oar in, thankful to have escaped the dreaded race, which was leaping and foaming at no great distance off in spite of the so-called hour of slack. It must be a great sight in a gale of wind; as it was, the waves dashed against each other with a crushing violence, sending the spray aloft in showers. Bad as Portland race undoubtedly is, a very small open dingy has been through it from end to end, on an average day, without shipping any water of importance; two men were lying down inside, and very wisely made no attempt to guide or row the little craft.

I stood into West Bay to guard against the race on the ebb, and then shaped a course for the Start, distant about fifty miles. The wind headed me when several miles off the land, and *The Kate* broke off towards Lyme Regis. The very light air could hardly drive the boat over the next flood, so that my progress was very slow, making it as late as 9 P.M. when I was off Bridport, where, being quite becalmed, I attempted to row in, and was about one mile off the harbour, when a gentle zephyr from the NE. disturbed the flag at the mast head. The oar was instantly used to turn the boat towards Lyme, which I made at 12.30 midnight. I had taken the precaution of rigging the boat with tiller lines, guessing that some one instance might occur in which they would be of the greatest service.

The distance from Bridport to Lyme is six miles, but the wind remained so provokingly light until my anchor was down that I was the whole three hours making the harbour. The lights are badly arranged, and the very points that need them most are left in utter darkness; namely, the outer pier and a beacon, on the remains of some architectural harbour disaster. The *Pilot Book* gives a mysterious direction as to how the lights should be kept; but the wording might mean anything, for the expression "Keep the lights open" makes no allowance for how much open. The exact wording should be "Keep the lights nearly in a line." But such a guide cannot always be depended upon, from the simple fact that it is not possible to keep the lights in the position wanted if beating to windward, consequently the dangerous points should be marked by a light, and the mariner be left to his own devices to keep clear, which, under such circumstances, would be easy enough.

I fastened on the tiller lines when within a half mile of the harbour, placed the anchor in readiness, and steered straight on from the bow, in hopes of being able to feel the way in somehow, for the night was pitch dark. I sighted the outer pier head, distant only a few yards, and instantly sheered to port, when, to my intense astonishment, a lofty post flew by, within an inch or two of the side, the bowsprit having just missed striking end on. I gave the boat room to swing clear as I hoped, and then plunged the anchor overboard; however, the iron keel took the rocks the whole way round, and I was obliged to shove off the beacon with the boat-hook. I was not furnished with proper side lights at that time, because I thought that any light would do. The riding light had been swinging about in the mizen rigging for the last two hours, so that a hand was off in a few minutes, who piloted the boat to a safe anchorage in the roadstead, for I refused to enter the harbour on hearing that the roadstead was a good one, because of the waste of time in getting out again in the morning.

The day had been a tiring one, and late as it was, I could not sleep without some refreshment; I therefore made tea, when a couple of hours' sleep completely restored my energies, rendering me fresh as a sparrow at 3 A.M. It blew a strong breeze through the night with frequent hard squalls, but the twenty pounds anchor did its work well, as did the rope-cable. The hand who left me at 1 A.M. promised to give me a call as he passed out to fish; however, I could not wait for him, but sent a half-crown to the care of the harbour-master at Lyme, to be given to the man who came off, and I can only hope he received it.

The fresh breeze carried me swiftly past Teignmouth and within six miles of Torquay, when, after knocking up a very considerable amount of sea, it left me almost becalmed, and several weary hours were passed beneath a burning sun with painful labour at the oar. Torquay is decidedly my favourite sea-side resort; so that, although a stranger to the place, I spent an hour cleaning up all my brass-work, and was not a little disappointed to find that, in spite of my exertions, it looked as dull the next day as if it had not been cleaned for a month. Brass-work is a source of great complaint, but the best varnish will protect it from the sea-air. I ate nothing throughout the day but a little bread, and breakfasted at the Imperial Hotel at the late hour of 6.30 P.M.

I may as well mention here that this was not an extraordinary hardship, but one of very frequent occurrence. Hardship is perhaps hardly the right word to use, for though one in appearance, to myself it could barely be called so, for I am easily satisfied in the eating line, and never require more than one good meal a day. The rules of my cuisine may be said to have consisted of tea about 4 A.M., with raw eggs; usually two in each cup, which would prove satisfying till about twelve mid-day, when a crust of bread or a few biscuits would carry me on till evening, when I either dined ashore or cooked a tin of preserved meat on board. The preserved meat is a very fine makeshift, but that is all I can say for it; and I should advise any one attempting a similar cruise to be careful and dine ashore as often as possible. The soup is very good, and the gravy from the meat tins is also very nourishing, but the meat itself is very ragged and much overcooked, but in no one single case did I ever taste the tin. I must say to the credit of Messrs. Morrell, of Piccadilly, that my stores were first-rate of their kind, the tea especially being very excellent.

I passed between the rocks of Torquay, and the tide threatened to put me first on one and then the other; but at last a breeze sprang up and took me safely in, but not till after severe punishment at the oar, the great stand-by in all difficulties. Dangerous places were avoided when there was any wind; but many are the hard fights I have had to keep off the rocks when becalmed in a tideway.

I put up at the Imperial Hotel, which is far more like a palace than a resting-place for the traveller. I think it is a question whether such hotels are wanted; for my part I candidly confess that I do not care about paying extravagant sums for other people's furniture and gorgeous architecture. The hotel in question is certainly well managed, but I should say badly placed, being right down by the water, instead of on the hillside, where it should be if intended to benefit invalids. Torquay appears to have a very healing air, said to be relaxing, but I cannot find out that it is more so in the heat of summer than that of other places. Its sea-bathing is the best I know of, the water being deep and beautifully clear, while the surrounding scenery makes it by far the most charming watering-place in England.

I was detained at Torquay in order to get the boat photographed and to fit the well with a tarpaulin which was to have been used whilst running in a heavy sea, but which was never once unrolled. The photographing was rather tedious work, as the sunlight was very fickle, and no amount of manœuvring would compel its glistening rays to court the creamy surface of the sails. Still, the photographs are, I consider, very satisfactory, and characteristic of the little boat.

I slept on board the boat on Sunday night, so as to be ready for an early start on Monday morning.

35

A heavy fog detained me for a couple of hours, but at 7.30 I started for Dartmouth. A perfect fleet of trawlers put out as I passed Brixham, fine smart vessels which sailed away from *The Kate*, but usually with a cheering word of some sort. The fog was tolerably thick all the time, sometimes completely hiding the land; the wind, which was dead ahead, freshened up into a smart breeze towards 11 o'clock, and I just saved my tide into the Dart. The coast from Berry Head is excessively rocky, and affords no shelter whatever when the wind is on the land. There are two channels into the harbour, both more or less surrounded with dangers, and the hazard of striking the rocks is increased by the eddy of the winds, which sometimes baffles all attempts at trimming canvas and renders the assistance of a pilot necessary. I made my own way in through the west channel, trusting to my light draught of water and the guidance of the *Pilot Book*. The Scotch and Irish harbours usually render assistance imperative, but most of our own can be entered single handed, when a waterman should be in instant attendance. A fisherman brought me to an anchorage some two hundred yards south of the landing place.

The wide anchorage of the Dart has a most inviting appearance, but in reality it is a difficult place to bring up in, for the currents are very strong, and run in all sorts of directions. I rode to the kedge anchor for the first night, and the boat went about a great deal, partly from the action of the tides, and in a great measure from the very heavy squalls that whistled down the gullies. I had understood that the depth was about three fathoms; but I threw the lead over in the morning, and found eleven; hailed a waterman in consequence, and after a consultation about the weather (which threatened to make me a prisoner) the boat was removed to the east anchorage and firmly moored with both anchors from the bow. To moor with both anchors from the bow, let go the large anchor and wait till the boat swings, then run out the small one nearly at right angles, taking care to fasten its cable on to the chain, which must be lowered for several feet. The fog in which I sailed from Torquay was but the precursor of a south-west gale and continual fog which lasted three days, and rendered it utterly impossible to round the Start from the east. I slept on board every night, but went to the Castle Hotel for meals. I grudged the delay at Dartmouth, but was recompensed in some measure by the natural beauty of the place, which gains its greatest charm, to my way of thinking, from the entrance of the harbour. I pulled some little distance up the river in the dingy, but the scenery appeared much tamer, and not nearly so beautiful as at the mouth.

CHAPTER IV

FROM DARTMOUTH TO ST. IVES

My aneroid stood high on Friday, the 9th of July, and as the morning was fine I made sail for Salcombe at 7.30. The breeze was very unsteady and accompanied by squalls. I was obliged to reef down in the bay, and it was lucky I did so, for a heavy squall struck me when near the Start, and *The Kate* had all her work to do to stand up, reefed as she was. A real Atlantic swell was running off the point—the famous ground sea, in fact—but not dangerous there, except when in a gale. It was glorious mounting the enormous waves, and then lurching down till nothing could be seen but the sky overhead. If any sea will make a man sick, the Atlantic swell will, for it gives such a send to the boat. There was not a single white crest to be seen, the sea being in fact as smooth as oil, but forced into successive massive swells, by atmospheric pressure commonly called a fog.

The wind had died away, or flung its spiteful vengeance on the bay, where curling seas might still be seen to dash the bitter tears of forced submission to the breeze. The sea was very lumpy about half way to Prawl Point, and changed from a swell to much more of a race character, being decidedly furious, and yet the race is said to be off the Start itself. The two points are very close, and races are so shifty that on the morning in question the commotion may have been further west than usual: whether such was the case or not, the water was very much smoother exactly opposite Prawl Point. I made up to some fishermen in Salcombe bay, who told me I would find sufficient water over the bar, towards which I steered, and was about a half mile off when, being nearly becalmed, I thought breakfast would be an agreeable change. The furnace was therefore put in order, a tin of meat prepared, a general negligence prevailing as to the direction of the fleet. I am not prepared to say how long this state of things may have lasted, when it suddenly occurred to me that the harbour was at least a mile off, the rocks to leeward unpleasantly adjacent, and the very light air dead ahead. The paddle cut the wave, the sheets were hauled, but still the flowing tide swept swiftly through the bay. *The Kate* was losing ground, because the tidal set was strongly on the rocks; I was just thinking of appealing to the anchor at the end of some two hours' distressingly hard work, when a smart head wind allowed the boat to beat off and enter the harbour. This was just about as unpleasant a fix as I could well have been placed in, for the bay is notoriously dangerous, several pleasure boats having been set on the rocks, according to my informant, who seemed a trustworthy man. In every case of the sort, if the paddle fails, the anchor must be cast, but that would have left the craft in a very risky position, for if instead of a smart breeze a fresh gale had sprung up, everything must have depended on the anchor, for that tide at least.

The harbour is a very difficult one to enter, on account of its narrow entrance and the very strong tide; but it affords excellent shelter when once inside. The best place for small yachts to bring up is on the right hand side opposite the town, and a small landing-place to the east usually marked by fishermen's boats. The anchorage is deep, being ten fathoms in, most places, and requires both anchors. Salcombe has enjoyed celebrity from having turned out very first class fruit ships. *The Kate* was much admired, and I received a very kind reception from the owner of the *Drift*.

I usually arranged the fire-place during the evening; swept the hearth; brightened the bars; walked up and down the chimney; laid the sticks and coal; filled the kettle and the tea-egg; placing sundry lumps of sugar in mysterious little corners. *Ergo*, at an early hour in the morning the application of the amount of fire usually conveyed in a match created a musical performance. The Russian bass led off in soft, melodious whispers, which increased to rushing roars of amorous affection and embraced his silent partner's boots, who, growing warm in turn, would breathe a plaintive air of soft, forbidding accents which would change to more permitting strains as heated charms o'ercame their mortal chains. Meanwhile a stirring strife! Miss Napkin tends the cup, then wooden fork pours lash on lash on would-be cocks and hens; the juice of that tall fruit, which grows on India's strand whose sweetened taste brought toothache in the world, the nigger's woe, with loss of Afric till one Yankee man restore them to fond liberty's round seat, is mingled with the bubbles that proclaim the water boils; what scene is there that can compare to my opera in the morning? *

I was towed out of the harbour at 5 A.M. on Saturday, and lay becalmed outside for two hours, during which time the paddle performed the duty of the breeze. It was rather risky work, keeping in the young ebb, as its channel was very narrow, and the coast very rocky. A nice breeze sprang up about NE., which carried me into Plymouth through the east entrance. I took a pilot when just outside the winter rocks, as the passage is narrow and dangerous. To be sure, it is marked by a buoy, but my experience tells me that it is not always possible to know on which hand to pass the buoy, the *Pilot Book* being usually eccentric in its information on this head. *The Kate* created its usual sensation, the Plymouth men observing that the expedition was a great undertaking for any man, even for a professional, with a thorough knowledge of the coast.

My pilot called me on Sunday at 3.50 A.M., and conducted the boat outside the winter rocks. The distance from the harbour to the breakwater is 3½ miles. I cannot say exactly how long I was getting under weigh, but I will allow half an hour. The breeze was NE., and very strong, as was the hot spring flood making into the harbour. The following times will give an idea of what the boat will do in a breeze proportioned to the canvas. The pace was not quite as good all the way as that out to the breakwater, for four reasons. In the first place, the harbour draught greatly added to the force of the true breeze; in the second, the tide was much stronger outside at the distance of several miles from the land than in the harbour;

* In his second edition he remarked that none of his critics observed that he was parodying Milton.

40

thirdly, the wind was occasionally light till clear of Rame Head; and, fourthly, the water was rough outside. The breakwater was passed at 4.50½ A.M., Rame Head at 5.45½ A.M., Zoe island at 7.10, after which a light air took me off Falmouth, and deserted me entirely some three miles from the harbour, into which I worked my way against the tide by sheer force of rowing, assisted, when inside, by a gentle breeze.

The rowing was uncommonly hard work on that day, as the water was very lumpy, inflicting many hard raps on the knuckles. On such occasions nothing but the most unflinching rowing wins the day; there must be no stopping to look at the time, no stopping to smoke a pipe, no stopping when tired, and none when distressed; hour after hour the paddle must force the boat over the stream until either a breeze or a position commands success. Position has an immense deal to do with working tides. If sailing for a harbour distant about two or three miles, and the favourable tide is at its last hour, keep well out, and let the tide carry the boat past the harbour as far as it will, when the return tide will put it in; whereas if you attempt to work inshore you will be certain to miss, and have to anchor for six hours until the next time. If you miss on the first plan, you can then work in and bring up. For my part I have rarely anchored, preferring to fight my way over the tide, the very idea of being obliged to submit being in itself positively hateful. Again, the time at which a harbour is made has a great deal to say to proceeding next day, and I take the liberty of thinking that the man who has to anchor for tides, from want of energy to drive the boat over them, will never succeed in getting round England, unless, indeed, in a most favourable season. To drive a boat with a ton and a half of ballast on board over a tide means to endure very severe punishment, as anyone can find out for himself, and yet it has to be done, day after day, beneath a broiling sun.

Falmouth is an easy harbour to make; the large vessels bring up all over the roads out of and in the tide way, although the stream makes at a great pace. I know no harbour which has such a grand appearance from the immense amount of vessels always riding at anchor: each ship an independent world. Small boats and yachts should pass the new harbour, and bring up in front of the town in about three fathoms.

My compass was made by Messrs. Dent, and was such as are used by the lifeboat institution. They have several faults, and mine acted in what might have been a way very dangerous to myself. In the first place, the compass is retained on the gimbals by one screw, the thread of which is too short, and is not received into a corresponding worm, so that in reality the action is not that of a screw but simply of a nail. In the second place, the door is not wide enough to allow of a broad hand to pass through, so that on each occasion when my compass required more spirit or was thrown off the gimbals I had (with one exception) to take it to a man for correction. Large air-bubbles had formed on the card, so that hearing Falmouth boasted a man skilled in compasses I took mine for his inspection. He pronounced it to be too slow, and in my then ignorance I agreed to his ideas of quickening the motion. To make a compass quicker or slower, remove the compass-card and sharpen or dull the point on which the card revolves. A difference quite imperceptible to the eye will greatly accelerate or retard the motion. The compass for a boat requires a sluggish movement, because the shortened keel enforces lively deviation from the track; and if the compass was as fast as that used by large vessels, its rapidity would cause a difficulty in reading for the simple reason that the shock or motion would be too powerful, the card rotating beyond the deviation of the boat. I received my compass from the seer towards evening, having paid a half-crown to have it rendered unserviceable; a fact I failed to discover till beating to windward off the Lizard.

I prepared to round that point on Monday, leaving my anchorage at 3 A.M. with a very light but favourable harbour draught. The flood was still making up, and as the breeze deserted me when opposite the new harbour I threw the kedge down and waited for the ebb or wind. To battle with the tide in Falmouth would have been an act of folly, for the crowd of ships at anchor compelled a careful course.

A fishing-boat made out of Falmouth, passed me while I

was at anchor, and brought up within a few yards, but within the new harbour. A conversation rapidly commenced between the two crews; when I discovered that they were going as far as the "Manacles," and offered to show me the shortest cut. We talked away for an hour or so, when the tide having slacked, we got our anchors and made off. There was not the smallest pretence of an air; so that we floated and paddled down to the "Manacles" bell-buoy. We had a long chat on the way; I received good advice, and returned pipes and light literature; both of which were thankfully accepted. The *World of Wonders Magazine* made me numberless friends. My after-locker had a very ample supply, the last numbers of which were distributed (if memory is correct) at Southwold, where even a gentleman standing by accepted one of *The Kate's* pamphlets.

If there is one book I like better than another, it is Aristotle's *Ethics*. I can assure the world at large that I am about the last man to care about publicity; I do not care one straw for praise; I would not care one straw if praise were purposely withheld, where there could be no doubt that it was my due. What do I want of my fellows? I want their esteem, their goodwill, but not their praise. What am I driving at? You will see. I have stated that I do not care about publicity; but I have wished before to-day to be a voice in my own nation, to be able to speak when I like, to hold my tongue when I like. Such is my idea of society, and I would associate with the nation; nothing less than the nation will please me. I have owned to a wish to be heard sometimes; and I will now state one of my reasons. I have observed that cheap editions of works have been issued by publishers of late years, such as *Shakespeare* and others; and I have yearned to call upon the publishers of this country to issue a cheap edition of Aristotle's *Ethics*, in large print, for the poor to read. I need say no more.

There was plenty of water for me inside of the bell-buoy, but as I had never seen one I passed just outside, about a yard or two distant. A very light head wind had sprung up so that I had to work into Coverack Bay; in doing so I ventured rather closer than was wise to the "Manacles" and found a different sort of tide. The oar as usual cleared all difficulties and I

brought up outside Coverack Harbour. A very strong breeze
sprang up about NNE. just as I was making the bay, offering
a great temptation to hold on, after having been becalmed,
but any further attempts in the direction of the Land's End
would have been useless against the strong flood. The breeze
very soon freshened into a gale, rendering it advisable to have
the boat towed into the harbour, a task which looked much
easier than it was. The boat chosen was much too light; the
consequence was that *The Kate* made a most determined set
towards the rocks, and I had to cast the heavy anchor to hold
her on their edge while another boat made fast. The second
boat dashed out instantly it was perceived what was happening,
thus reflecting great credit on the Coverack seamen. Ah, well,
sailors are rather different to others, and fishermen are the
very cream of sailors, a splendid body of men whose daily
calling couples rapid thought with instantaneous action;

The handle to the hammer head!

The wind kept on increasing, and during the night it blew
a strong gale. I collected the various opinions as to my chance
of making a point in Mount's Bay on the morning of July 13;
the sum being in favour of the attempt, because the bay affords
many chances with the wind off the land. The *Pilot's Handbook*, p. 10, gives the following description—"Mount's Bay has
five tidal harbours, viz. Mousehole, New Lyn, and Penzance on
the west side, Mount St. Michael at the head, and Port Severn
on the east side, but they all dry out at low water and none
should be attempted with onshore gales. Guavas Lake is in
the north-west part of the bay, and both it and the inner part
of the bay afford good summer anchorage except with winds
between SSW. and SE. which send in a very heavy breaking
sea, but the powerful under-tow (as in Torbay) enables a
vessel to ride easy in east and south-east gales. There is good
anchorage on the east shore of the bay off the north-west side
of the Mullion Island in ten fathoms with the island bearing
S. ½ E. and Mullion Ch. E. ¾ S., also in seven fathoms SSW.
one mile from Loopool and in eleven fathoms off Port Severn
with Helstone Ch., NE. by E., and Luddon Point NW., but
be prepared if the wind should shift suddenly to the west."

44

It will appear from the above that with a good chart marking all the anchorages a small boat might be safely berthed somewhere, even if a port could not be made. I bought a chart of the " Lizard," and I believe I am right in calling it an Admiralty sheet, judging from the names of its compilers. The tides round the " Lizard" run from three to four knots an hour; the above chart puts down the imbecile rate of $1\frac{1}{2}$ to $\frac{1}{2}$ a knot, and does not mark one single anchorage; consequently, had anything happened I must have trusted entirely to my own νοῦς.

Few but seamen know or ever realise the immense amount of danger that surrounds the vessel coasting Britain's iron shores. Let the *Pilot Book* speak again, at page 11: "Dangers. The following are the principal dangers to avoid in approaching the west side of Mount's Bay from the south Tregiftian rock, of 4 feet water, lying $\frac{1}{2}$ mile west from Tetterdu Point, Buck Rocks cover at one-third flood at 2 cables from Tetterdu Point. Haver Rock covers at quarter flood off Carndu Point. Jelland Rock covers at quarter flood at 2 cables east of Carndu Point. Low Lee Rock of 4 fathoms water, and steep-to, lies three-quarter mile east of Pen Lee Point, and is marked by a red buoy moored 30 yards east of the rock. Carn Base Rock at one-third mile north of Low Lee, has 4 feet water and steep-to. Gear Rock at $\frac{1}{2}$ mile S. by W. $\frac{3}{4}$ W. from Penzance Light House, covers at one-third flood, and is marked by an iron beacon. Cressar Raymond and Hokus ledges extend from the head of Mount's Bay, the former and latter running off one-third mile, the Raymond half mile. The south extreme of the Cressar covers at two-third flood; on their west limit is an iron red beacon, surmounted by a ball. Guthen Rock of 10 feet water, lies a long cable off the west shore of the Mount, and WNW. from its castle. Maltman Rock covers at one-quarter flood at 1 cable off shore and SW. $\frac{1}{4}$ S. from the Castle. The following rocky shoals are on the East of Mount's Bay. Boa, of 6 fathoms water, breaks heavily in SW. gales at 3 miles NW. by W. from the Lizard and Rinsey Head; Great Row, of 3 fathoms water, and foul uneven ground on all sides, lies 1 mile SW. by W. from the Wellor, and $2\frac{1}{4}$ miles off Cuddan Point;

Irongates, of 4 fathoms water, lies 2 miles SW. $\frac{1}{2}$ S. from Cuddan Point; Mountamopus, of 5 feet water, lies three-quarter mile south of Cuddan Point, and a black buoy marks its south edge; Carn Mallows, of 3 fathoms water, is half-mile south-east of Mountamopus." Now, reader, how would you like to face that lot for the first time in your life and utterly alone, in a strong top-gallant breeze? with spray cutting the eyes almost out of your head, and every danger increased by the fact of being obliged to beat to windward, thereby creating a wonderful complication of bearings and difficulties from north, south, east, and west; those from any one quarter offering a sufficiently intricate problem. However, you may take my word for it that, bad as it looks, *The Kate* has sailed through many worse.

It was high water at the Lizard on July 13 at 10.32 A.M.; at Penzance at 7.12; at Falmouth at 8.12. The Coverack men count their high water much the same as that at the Lizard. The wind had moderated from what it had been during the night, but I was advised to put a double reef in the mainsail, as the off-land breeze has a trick of culminating vigour in Mounts Bay.

I started about 9 A.M., and ran before a strong breeze NNE. to the Lizard, passing through first the race off Blackhead and then that off the Lizard. A large full-rigged ship was a very considerable distance ahead, but the tide gave me the advantage, so that when off the Stags I was very little, if anything, astern; but I consider I picked up some distance by pure seamanship, for when round Blackhead I hauled up nearly three points, to escape being embayed, and thus made a straight course; whereas the big ship was being swept down towards me at a very rapid pace, thereby fast losing ground.

NNW. is the bearing course from the Lizard to Penzance, but the run of the tide around the coast of England often sets bearing courses at defiance. The tides from the Lizard to the Mount are excessively eccentric, requiring a careful study of two or three years, so that it would be folly for me to presume to determine their many winding ways.

I hugged the land as closely as possible after rounding the

Stag Rocks, making short tacks so as to avoid being swept off by the racing ebb which makes with the main stream towards the Land's End. I worked close up to the Mullion Rock, where I hove to and shook one reef out of the mainsail, as the wind appeared to have lulled a little. However, it very soon came on again with very sharp squalls, which repeatedly put two or three planks of the deck under.

Three large ships were working up some two or three miles ahead, not in a straight line but with regard to the distance *The Kate* must have travelled to reach them if they had brought up suddenly. These vessels worked close into the land, and I did the same, but passed them just after they had brought up. I do not suppose that any one of the three could be called a smart vesssel, certainly not the last, which I left about one mile astern, measured as above.

I discovered during the beat to windward that the compass was flying about in all directions and utterly useless in a sea-way, which fact determined me to make Penzance instead of St. Michael, or Mouse Hole, arguing that the number of in-habitants would be in proportion to the number of houses, that the number of wants would be in proportion to the number of inhabitants, and that any particular cure should be sought amid a crowd of wants.

I was perfectly soaked by the clouds of spray which the boat hove over me as she raced through the crisp hard seaway, for I kept her well full. The sheets were all made fast, but I sat to leeward with one hand on the tiller and the other on the jib sheet, so that had the emergency arisen I could have let it go instantly. By the time that I arrived at Penzance my face and blue Norfolk jacket were both white with the salt, as they have been many times since then.

I was speaking to the captain of the *Stella* yacht a few days ago when at Harwich. He was making the tour of England east about, while I went west about. The *Stella* was some-where off the Cornish coast in the breeze of the 13th, and the captain informed me he had as much as he could bear with a double-reefed mainsail and a storm foresail.

The compass was put to rights, and the next day I started

about 1 P.M. for St. Ives, but was becalmed off the Runnel Stone and had to row round to Sennen Cove, where some Land's End fishermen towed *The Kate* to a proper anchorage. Sennen Cove is small but deep, and affords excellent shelter to small craft (even in heavy gales) if brought up in the right place: remember that little point, reader, for it makes all the difference. The Land's End population took the greatest interest in *The Kate*, the women even sending one of their number. What corner of the earth, what strip of land, can boast more honest and heroic band than smiling Sennen Cove?

I weighed anchor at 1 P.M. on July 15, with a light air north by east, but was becalmed off the Brizzies and paddled to Gurnard's Head, when a fair wind took me in with labour at the oar. It was a very touch and go business making St. Ives, but so it was making any amount of other places that I arrived at on the ebb. It was such a near thing that the St. Ives pilots, seeing my difficulty, dashed out to assist, and were not a little put out because I persisted in entering before I would allow any one on board, as had been my custom all along the coast, where I saw a fair chance of doing so without injury to my own craft or the property of others. However, they gave me all the best advice in their power, and increased my geographical lore by information of the Bowling Canal, which they said was much better suited to my purpose than the Caledonian, fixed on simply because I was not aware of any other.

The navigation around the north coast of Scotland is of the very simplest kind, and offers a very fair field for the canoeist, but the eddy winds render it a very unprofitable cruising-ground for the yachtsman. There are a few strong races here and there, but such need not be approached; the general force of the tides being about one knot. The bugbear of the west coast is the Coriebhreacan, between the islands of Jura and Scarba. The flood makes straight for it, from the Crinan Canal, and if any one wants to commit a novel suicide let him venture through, in any ordinary sailing craft, after the first hour's flood or ebb, kindly giving a week's notice to sensation-hunting humanity, who can crown the heights on either side, and send

48

him below with a cheer. The tide rushes through the Sound at the rate of eight knots an hour, but, then, there is not the smallest necessity to pass within anything like a dangerous distance. If sailing northward out of the Crinan Canal, keep to the east of the islands, but if becalmed on the west side, anchor. There are any number of creeks on the way to the Orkneys, which one and all offer the very best anchorage; in fact, the whole place is an anchorage, and there are very few, if any, sunken rocks. The Pentland Firth is the terror of the north; the tide sweeps along seven and eight knots an hour, in several directions, making a tremendous race. But that may be avoided by passing through the Orkneys, where the tides average about one knot. Of course there is great danger of being swept through the Firth when crossing to the north and south, but this, like every other danger, can be met by a little common sense. In all such positions wait for a wind, and start on the half tide against.

CHAPTER V

FROM ST. IVES TO NEW QUAY

I DINED at the Western Hotel on Thursday evening, about 9 P.M., it being very late before I made the harbour; my log-book informs me that I entered bachelor-banishment at 12 midnight, and emerged at 2 A.M. as fresh as a moonbeam. A nasty fog detained me for the day, so that I studied life in St. Ives from the window of the Western Hotel and the piers. I was strongly advised of the sluggishness of man and the active energy of the horse, when looking out of the window on to the dull, dirty street. A cart, carter, and a horse stood below; a large jar was on the pavement. The carter, an idle-looking fellow, stood for some ten minutes talking to the boots, the horse showing the greatest disgust at the delay, telling its master as plainly as possible to put the jar into the cart and be off. The speechless conversation was carried on by looking in the most good-tempered manner at the jar, and then making pretence to bite the carman or the boots, and by frequent expressions of disgust, displayed by a rapid laying back of the ears and an angry champing of the bit; the greatest delight being shown when the jar was deposited in its proper place.

I took the opportunity of delay to write up my log, which, I may as well mention, was never written on board, for the simple reason that the necessary conveniences did not exist, nor did the time; and doubtless the narration of the cruise has suffered to a considerable extent, for to do justice to the intense toil, the continued hardship, actual distress, and the many critical positions, is not in the power of a cold-blooded writer; the time has flown, and winged description's pen.

I may say, in self-defence, that I had not the slightest intention of publishing a book on the subject, for many reasons. In the first place, it is not pleasant writing of one's self; secondly, I had a strong dislike to publish any prose composition; but thirdly, I have been engaged for more than two years in the production of an arduous literary labour. The work has nearly killed me once, and the cruise in *The Kate* was undertaken simply to gather strength for its continuation, consequently I grudged all further tax on my resources, and have written this work because every one appeared to wish it.

I had hoped to get round much sooner than I did, but was fully prepared for the fatiguing time that the voyage eventually occupied. I have been repeatedly asked if it was absolutely necessary to be so long. I answer that, under the conditions of weather, weight of boat, amount of canvas, want of experience, and my utter ignorance of the road, the time into Yarmouth was such that I would not start again and undertake to beat it. Yet there is no reason why the tour should not be made in half the time under favourable conditions. But even with fine weather and a flowing sheet all the way, I doubt any man being able to go every day. I know that my own energies were taxed to the very utmost, and they have often been severely tried before; but it should be remembered (as stated later on) that I was in very bad health when I started.

I believe I am the only man who has ever walked what may be called an international race with the natives of India. A discussion arose at the mess-table about the powers of endurance of an Indian and an Englishman in India, the odds of two to one being offered against any man at the table who would make a match against a certain native to walk from Umritsur into Meean Meer, about thirty-three miles. The match was nearly falling through, when I, who had been a quiet but most indignant listener to the dispute, offered to walk the man, allowing others to make what bets they liked, but starting myself for honour only. I had never walked a match, and was ignorant of the full extent of my powers in that line; still I had something to go upon, in that the three different schools I was at could not produce a runner of about my own age who could beat me, at either long or short distances. I had a bad knee from the effects of football and having been shot by a bullet, my knee being a very treacherous member to the present day. I was completely out of training, as the saying is (though I never require to train for anything), so that the odds were very fairly against me, the native being a smart fellow, in capital condition.

The match was made, to the best of my remembrance, on a Friday evening, and walked off on the following Monday morning. I forget the date, but I know it was one of the hottest days in the year; the dust was three or four inches deep on the road, from the fact of there having been no rain for nearly three months. I borrowed a pair of shoes for the occasion, having only regimental boots of my own. The start was at 4 A.M., from the cross-roads at Umritsur to the gardens at Meean Meer. A heel and toe match would have been nonsense, because neither walkers nor judges could have written a correct essay on the subject, consequently we were to cover the ground how we could. The native started off to cut me down, but I soon found I could compel him to run every now and then so as to keep up: at the end of twenty miles he was beaten, though he certainly walked as gamely as any man could, being some fifty yards ahead of me at the commencement of the last mile, a distance I had allowed him to gain to get him on, knowing I could pass at any moment. The whole distance was covered in five hours and forty minutes, from which at least fifteen minutes should be cut, for I waited four times on the road for my friend to drink, his caste preventing his liquor being carried by anyone, while mine was conveyed in a small flask by one of the officers of the regiment, so that instantly I saw my opponent stop to drink, my notions of fair play compelled me to wait for him; in fact, the last time I waited not only for him to drink, but until he was fit to go on, as he at that period (some five miles from the end) said he could go no further, and I am sure he deserved a medal for walking the next four miles.

At the end I rode my horse bare-backed into Meean Meer, a distance of three miles, rising to the trot as if I had stirrups. My saddle, by some mistake, was not there; however, stirrups were not of much account at that time. I remember once, when on duty, turning out guard on a grey pony I was riding for the first time, having borrowed it for the occasion. It had a dislike to red-coats or bayonets, as many Indian horses have, and I had great difficulty to get it near the place. It was a noted rearer, and on that occasion it reared up perfectly straight, and both my stirrups fell off. I turned out the guard and rode a considerable distance before I discovered that my saddle gear was not complete, on which I returned and recovered the stirrups. The guard in question was the hospital guard at Meean Meer, and doubtless some of the men are still in the regiment and remember the fact, especially as the night was very dark, and the guard lamp had to be brought out to lessen the difficulty of finding the lost articles.

The damage to my knee arose in the first instance in the following manner. I rushed at the football and kicked it exactly at the same second that another but much heavier boy kicked. The pace of my rush was such that it knocked my opponent as flat as a pancake, and I do not doubt that he remembers it to the present day, for it certainly appeared to me that his head bounced off the ground from the force of the concussion. The ball spun straight up in the air, and was falling just behind me to the left, when I caught sight of it, twisted suddenly round to kick with my right, and threw the left knee out of the socket; it flew back, and I went on playing. The knee brought me to grief four times before the final catastrophe, when I was knocked down, my knee being wrenched round and five heavy fellows on top of me, after which, being barely able to crawl, I gave up playing. I was laid up for three months with an enormous knee, and was attended by the present Dr. Wills, of Jersey. I had no sooner recovered when I met with another accident, being shot exactly under the same knee by a pistol bullet, which was cut out of the left side of the thigh. The bullet slipped when cut down upon, rendering it necessary that some one should hold the flesh firmly on each side while the second incision was being made. The necessary pressure was made by myself. My knee has frequently gone since then; very nearly gave in my walking match in India, and spoke very plainly when I was off Whitby, that it would not stand any more rowing.

The *Rob Roy* book presented the idea of a cruise, and I grasped it instantly, as a dying man grasps a straw, and I am certain that no less excitement would have pulled me round.

I started a wretched, worn-out scribbler, weighing 10 st. 4 lbs., and returned a hearty man of 11 st., the greatest weight I have ever attained. Talk about change of air! Well, doubtless even that is good, but what people want is a change of life—a fresh excitement to divert the wretched routine of ideas which haunt the stagnant brain, or else to check the ceaseless craving of the active mind.

The power of exhausting is the certain mark of first class mental ability. Give me the man who is sick to death of everything (remember the everything, reader, for without his food he cannot be sick), who loved but has exhausted hunting, shooting, fishing, and the whole routine of manly sports at twenty-five or thereabouts; that man is sure to have a fund of greatness, and in proportion to such fund is his chance of leaving an honourable mark on the world. It is necessary to put in the word honourable, because some people imagine they can leave their mark in marble, granite, bricks, or other stone, and so they do, but one which often proves disastrous to the child.

I spent an hour in the evening watching the youth of St. Ives fishing from the pier. At least one hundred children, from five to twelve years of age, were seated or stood upon the edge which overlooks the water at a height sufficient to ensure death if any rolled over. Each was armed with a fishing-line, which he contrived to jerk out to its full length, with his legs dangling over the side or standing finely balanced on the edge. The wall slants out toward the sea, rendering a clear fall into the water quite impossible, so that any unfortunate would have the pleasure of drowning with a broken limb or two. I confess I felt rather humiliated, for a perfect crowd of children were doing what I would not have tried under at least a week's practice of looking over, so as to acquire the necessary steadiness.

The power of looking over a height is very peculiar. Perhaps medical men will inform us what nerve it affects. I have stood for a half hour at a time looking out on the main royal yard of the ship *Albemarle* when the sail was hoisted, but I would not attempt to get near the yard now, and yet I suppose I am the same individual, and I know I am bolder as I am older. The courage of a lad is akin to rashness, because he does not analyse his position, whereas the man is intellectually brave, and takes a calm survey of possible contingencies.

I was prepared for a start at 3.30 A.M. on the morning of Saturday, July 17, but awaited the tide till 5.30. A description of the work on this day may be taken as a specimen of the labour required to round the Cornish coast. The bay of St. Ives is about as dangerous a place as a stranger can wish to find himself in, for sunken rocks run out from Godrevy Head for a very great distance. There is a very narrow passage between the lighthouse, situated on a rock off the head, and the rocks outside, but it should never be attempted by a stranger, and by one acquainted only with a fresh fair wind. The inside passage cuts off some two or three miles of the distance to Padstow, so I determined to chance it, depending entirely on my powers of rowing the boat should the wind fail.

The great danger in all narrows arises from the force of the tide and its various currents, twisting the boat first one way and then the other. To say the tide flows so many miles an hour will convey no earthly idea to many minds, so let me compare a three-knot stream to the Thames between Hampton Court and Surbiton after a week's summer rain, or to what I take to be the pace of most English rivers during a summer flood. The reader who is not a yachtsman or a mathematician will be able to form an idea of the force of the stream by walking along the bank, but only practical experience will teach him the difficulty of handling a three ton boat with one oar in such a current; all other difficulties aggravated, as often as not, by lumpy water, and an almost imperceptible breath of air, which takes the sails aback, and renders the labour as heavy again.

I left St. Ives with a very slight land breeze from the SE., which in a most provoking manner took me within a half mile of the lighthouse, and then left me entirely to my own devices. The flood had commenced to make up, so that an attempt to round the reef would have placed the boat on it to a certainty. I was therefore compelled to choose between anchoring or attempting the passage called the Narrows. To touch a rock was most likely to lose the boat by being upset by the stream or knocked to pieces by the seaway. The oar decided the matter as usual, and I got through after a half-hour as hard work as I ever had in my life. My instructions had been to keep as close to the light as possible, but, although I rowed in the most determined manner directly for the lighthouse, the powerful tide swept me steadily down towards the reef, keeping me hard at work for at least half-a-mile on the other side before I could consider the boat out of danger. A reef of rocks appears to draw the stream towards it, both from the tide side and right and left, a fact I noticed particularly when off the dangerous race of the Three Stones Oar. I took great pains to keep clear of it, because it sets right down on to the rocks.

I should say *The Kate* was at least one mile outside the Stones, and the flood should have been carrying me on to St. Ives, when, to my astonishment, the land showed me clearly that I was going back again; in fact, some tidal eccentricity was sweeping me back towards the rocks. The paddle cut the difference, but the lesson was never forgotten. I started at 5.20, with a light air and hardly any tide. The distance to the lighthouse was about three miles; I will therefore calculate it was about 7 A.M. when I had worked clear of the reef which I will call sweat No. 1, say a two-pounder.

The paddle being laid aside, I will take the liberty of imagining that I smoked a pipe. The important event is not logged, but that I sighted the *Maria Betsey* is, and that the oar was again put out, and a stern chase commenced, which ended by my getting alongside about half a mile to the southward of Paltreith. Captain Williams, of the coaster, pointed out the harbour, which I instantly made for, so as to clinch my advance, and to avoid being put on the reef by the return tide, or again compelled to pass the Narrows. I worked on till close in, when a strong harbour draught coaxed me on to St. Agnes, and ended sweat No 2, which I will call a one-pounder.

The harbour draught failed me before I got to St. Agnes' Head, so that the paddle commenced again, and took me in towards that anchorage. The tide nearly put me on to the

big rocks known as the "Man and his Man"; they are perfectly steep-to, and the boat's side might have touched them
except for the surf, which would have caused some damage, no
doubt, from the violence of the shock. For instance, the bowsprit or the mizen-boom might have been snapped, and have
caused detention at the next port, so that, all things considered,
I think I was wise in battling with the tide until the harbour
draught from St. Agnes swept me on towards New Quay, and
ended sweat No. 3, which I will call another pounder.

The sun was burning hot, and the heat may be guessed from
the fact that the continued glare had rendered my left eye
utterly useless, and had compelled me to buy a pair of coloured
glasses at St. Ives. The best sort were not procurable, but I
found a common pair, without side-laps, of the very greatest
service. A lovely breeze was blowing me along, in company
with one or two other coasters and a yacht from New Quay. I
was hesitating whether I would venture inside of Carter's Rock,
when, without a second's warning, a head-wind settled the
question for the moment, and compelled me to stand outside.
The shift of the wind is most astonishing, though, strictly speaking, "shift" does not describe the movement on that occasion,
which in fact was a shift of the boat out of one fresh current of
air into another from exactly the opposite direction, the old
current remaining as it was, and bringing up a vessel astern,
which on reaching the barrier was taken aback exactly as I
had been. The head-wind lasted a very short time, and left
us all at the mercy of the ebb, which was making past Carter's
Rock in great strength, although there was little or no tide
inside, a fact I was not aware of at the time. I determined, as
usual, that I would not go back if I could help it.

I was about a quarter of a mile to the south-east of Carter's
Rock. A fishing-boat was brought up north-west of it. My
campaign was formed instantly—to force the boat over the
tide, and make fast to the fishing-boat. The oar was put out,
and with the assistance of a light air I stood close up to the
rock, when, to my intense disgust, away went the light air, and
away I went astern. However, true to myself and the game of
chance, I fought for every inch; but back I went the full

quarter of a mile, when again a gentle puff set me right up to the rock. The next tack was the awkward one, because the boat would then be right across the stream. I paddled as hard as I could, after having gone about, and just shaved a large coaster which had been ahead, but was then dropping rapidly back with the tide. Of course I lost ground on that tack, but made sufficient westing to fetch the west corner of Carter's Rock on the return.

I was getting rather used up, as may be guessed, and went about, also astern again, but put about instantly I thought I could clear the big rock, and headed for the fishing-boat. To head for an object in a tideway is to miss it, which I did by some thirty yards, when I again stood out for a final effort, went about as soon as the fisherman sang out, made fast alongside, and lay down perfectly exhausted. Thus ended sweat No. 4, which I will call any amount of pounders.

Now, the whole of this work was done on a couple of cups of tea, with two eggs beat up in them, a small bit of bread, and a pipe or two. I had not tasted a drop of liquor, because the heat of the sun was something fearful. The fishermen gave me a couple of Cornish buns, which I ate with great relish, and washed them down with a glass of sherry, after they had drunk the boat's health. And now, reader, perhaps you imagine the day's work over. Not a bit of it. I had to row the boat nearly the whole distance into New Quay.

I remained alongside the fishing-boat for about two hours, when, the tide having slacked, the men in it rowed off for New Quay, and I followed, eventually making that harbour late in the day. Thus ended sweat No. 5. And now perhaps my readers may begin to understand what it is to take a three-ton boat round England, remembering that this sketch will suit for many other days.

CHAPTER VI

ON HARBOURS OF REFUGE

THE south-west coast of Cornwall is excessively exposed, and requires a large harbour of refuge. The Bristol Channel and the Welsh coast have a few good roadsteads, but not a single good harbour that vessels may run for in heavy gales. Milford Haven offers splendid protection when once inside, but vessels are not recommended to attempt it in dirty weather, for the tides run with such velocity that it is almost impossible to be certain of hitting the entrance. The *Pilot Book* for the St. George's Channel (published by Charles Wilson, of London), at page 2, reads as follows: "Milford Haven. This is the only safe harbour for a large ship between the Land's End and Holyhead. It is the most secure and commodious harbour in England, and may be entered without a pilot, either by day or by night, even with contrary winds, only taking the tide. Vessels may, without either anchor or cable, run ashore within it with complete safety on a bed of soft ooze in Angle Bay; but in thick weather nothing but absolute necessity should induce anyone to run for it."

> Defessi Æneadæ quæ proxima litora cursu
> Contendunt petere, et Libyæ vertuntur ad oras.
> Est in secessu longo locus; insula portum
> Efficit, objectu laterum, quibus omnis ab alto
> Frangitur, inque sinus scindit sese unda reductos.
> Hinc atque hinc vastæ rupes, geminique minantur
> In cœlum scopuli, quorum sub vertice late
> Æquora tuta silent; tum sylvis scena coruscis
> Desuper, horrentique atrum nemus imminet umbrâ.
> Fronte sub adversâ scopulis pendentibus antrum:
> Intus aquæ dulces, vivoque sedilia saxo
> Nympharum domus: hic fessas non vincula naves
> Ulla tenent: unco non alligat ancora morsu.
> —*Æneidos* i. 157–169.

TRANSLATION.

The weary Trojans seek the nearest shore,
And gain the Libyan coast where billows roar
Against an isle that guards an inland bay
Where wooing currents wend their winding way;

THE CRUISE OF THE KATE

Where beetling cliffs, two twin-like rocks oppose
Their towering fronts, and ward the tempest's blows;
A sylvan scene adorns the dizzy height;
A gloomy grove refracts a softened light
On grots, and cooling springs within a cave
Where nymphs resort to dabble in the wave,
And smile protection, that the vessels ride.
Without the anchor's bite, the cable's guide.

No less than ten ships went ashore near St. Ann's Head on the same night during one of the late winters. The whole ten were under the impression that they were making Dale Roads, which is but a very little distance on the right hand, and offers an excellent anchorage. They sailed in single file, and struck one on top of the other, only two or three hands escaping to tell the tale. Such a catastrophe could never have happened had minute guns been fired from St. Ann's Head. Lighthouses are excellent things in their way, but lights and friendships fade.

There is excellent anchorage between Carter's Rock and the Chick Rocks, and the space would make a capital harbour. Breakwaters should be run out from each of these rocks, taking care to leave a wide entrance. Others might be run right across from the Man and his Man Rocks, converting the whole bay to the Chick into a capital harbour of refuge. Vessels might not be able to recover their anchors in some parts, but that is better than losing the ship and crew. The bay of St. Ives would also make an excellent harbour if protected by a breakwater.

It is quite a disgrace to a wealthy country like this that such little care is shown for the lives of seamen who form its chief bulwark. The expense of building harbours is usually thrown on the locality or on the shipping world, as if the inland manufacturers and the wealth of the country did not depend on the successful commercial traffic on the sea. Property is lost every year, which forms a very large and continued drain on the resources of the country, and would well repay the outlay by the Government of sums for the building of harbours. Those that exist are in most instances useless to vessels exceeding a few hundred tons, from the fact of the piers being very much too close together, compelling the commanders of large ships to keep the sea rather than run the risk of being smashed against a pier. Many of them have their entrances on the wrong side, as that of Whitby, for instance, which faces a very dangerous rock. The brilliant hotels at Scarboro', the fashionable parade, and the carefully laid out terraces afford a very unpleasant contrast to the wretched protection offered seamen in the shape of a harbour; and yet mere pleasure is in one scale and the risk of life in the other. Such things do not reflect credit on the national social economy, nor do they convey the idea of the different interests taking a pride in each other's welfare, but figure as the peculiar marks of bad government, for if the selfishness of men prevent their acting honestly by each other, it is the particular duty of the Government to see that no legitimate interest suffers for the benefit of another. To build a breakwater is by no means an easy matter, and all ordinary difficulties would be much increased by the ground swell on the Cornish coast. It may be worth while for engineers to consider the possibility of floating one, which would answer the required purpose of breaking the seas, if sunk within a few feet of the bottom. The necessity for a breakwater appearing above the surface at all may be fairly questioned, for a sunken reef makes an excellent breakwater, as any engineer may satisfy himself about by passing six months or a less period at anchor in the natural harbour of Boulmer, about seven miles north of Coquet Island, on the coast of Northumberland. If the breakwaters are continued above the surface, to break the wind as well as the sea, why should they not be hives of busy bees, and thus pay their own expenses? I take it a line of our old hulks would make a very fair breakwater, but vessels could be built exactly to suit the purpose. The opening between each ship would have a good effect, as legitimate thoroughfares for wind and sea; lessening the pressure on each vessel, which should be pierced with as many tubes as could possibly be arranged, to allow the tide to flow through, steadying the craft, and taking the strain off the moorings.

There is little or no tide after the first two hours in the bay between the Chick and Man rocks, so that the yacht, which had drifted a long way astern, had worked up again with a light wind and passed *The Kate* before I cast off from the fishing-boat. The large coasters were not so lucky, but were swept completely out of mind; that is, I saw them no more, and had they been visible, I think I would have noticed their position. Of course I had no chance of keeping pace with the cloud of delicate muslin, *The Kate* liking short petticoats, so that her joints may work freely, but rounded, leathered, feathered pine made such an excellent topsail that the yacht was caught.

Its pleasure-party from New Quay were fishing for mackerel with hooks and lines, and, like many other people, expressed surprise that *The Kate's* larder was not replenished in the same way. I suppose few men have had better fishing than I have; it was the one sport I cared most about, but now I do not know that I could bring myself to kill a fish, shoot a bird, or indulge in any killing sport whatever. I like to see the world swimming, flying, jumping, or otherwise engaging itself, for God knows there is enough misery to be seen without the wriggle of the fish, the flutter of the bird, or the dying challenge of the stag. There is a pleasure far above any that the sportsman can ever feel, and that is to live and let live. I can sit and watch the enjoyment of animal life for hours. I see a horse trotting with its noble air of freedom around its pasture; I become a part of that horse; I know exactly what it is thinking about, and I share its pleasures. I see a swallow rejoicing in the sunshine and its power of wing; I become a part of that swallow; its pleasures are my pleasures, its pains are my pains. I see a snail creeping along, with its house on its back; I watch that snail; I become part of that snail; I learn to be patient, humble, and enduring. I learn to do, for I see that, however slow the doing, it may have a direct aim, and that such direct aim can only be reached by such peculiar, untiring slowness. I am watching the snail; it is crossing a road; it is in danger. Do I take it up and carry it over? No, because I understand that that animal must work after its own peculiar instincts, and if I was to move it too quickly, the effect would be much the same as if a violent gale had blown me into the Atlantic, leaving me without a notion of where I was, or any other method of finding out but by sailing back again. Human beings must have food, and therefore inferior animals must be killed, but necessity alone should be the death-warrant, for cannibalism may return without special licence.

The invention of steam, and the further invention of machinery, has appeared to the poor, especially to the labouring poor, as a peculiar hardship, depriving them of the means of subsistence; but in reality every new machine, every saving of labour, other than that of man, increases the stock of animal food for the human race, for it is plain that if we had to work our bullocks we should not have so many to eat, and meat would be dearer in consequence; it is also plain, that as agriculture means science, and science means time, from the imitation of lightning to a culmination in literary art, so the gain in time allows the field to be better prepared, yields the larger crop, and cheapens vegetable food, which is all a direct gain for the poor.

CHAPTER VII

FROM NEW QUAY TO BOSCASTLE

THE slight breath of wind had died away, and left the two crafts in company just off the Chick Rock. I had a chat with the sailing master of the pleasure-boat, and then pursued my way to New Quay in what is called a stalk calm. A fresh head-breeze met me just east of the entrance to the harbour, which was made about 8 P.M., the yacht being rowed along about one mile in rear. The country above Carter's Rock appears from the water to offer a fine site for a town, which would enjoy a most commanding sea-view.

The harbour at New Quay is small, and, like all the Cornish harbours, is perfectly dry at low-water. Why are the harbours on this coast, as on the north-east coast of Great Britain, for the most part tidal? On examination, the answer appears in the shape of the surf-sea that runs to a greater or less extent on each, and conveys the idea that vessels are considered safer on dry land than in the water when a surf-sea is running. Such must have been the radical idea, and may be found to answer very well in some harbours; but in many the shipping suffers most at low-water, when the ground-sea rushes in to a depth of eight feet, and returns with the force of a torrent, smashing every vessel in the place to pieces. It stands to reason that, if harbours had been formed in places which always afford a considerable depth of water, the rush of the sea would have been lessened by the opposition of the body in the harbour, and the fearful return could not take place at all. I see no reason why the whole inlet at New Quay should not be made into an excellent harbour of refuge. A stone breakwater in the shape of a redan might be built, and would have a better chance of standing than one placed at right angles to the sea. A few hulks anchored outside would afford protection while the redan was being built. If stone will not answer, some other material will. A redan dock, for instance, at once a breakwater and a harbour. A sand running nearly parallel to the coast affords a very excellent roadstead as long as the wind is from the land or sand side. The only question as to our power of imitating the action of the sand lies in the problem, whether a surface stoppage will break the sea sufficiently to allow of vessels riding safely behind it.

It would be worth while to form a large roadstead somewhere off the Cornish or north-east coasts of Great Britain, as an experiment. A line of vessels, drawing some forty or fifty feet and about fifty yards in beam, might form a three-sided roadstead, offering a protection from every quarter, and leaving three wide entrances. If it was found to answer, a small charge on each vessel would very soon pay expenses.

A fog detained me on Sunday, July 18. I therefore seized the opportunity and took my washing ashore, to have the extreme pleasure of bringing it all back again, because it was Sunday and the washerwoman obstinate.

A large crowd assembled to see the boat in the afternoon, the rail being completely occupied from stem to stern, while others stood around, three and four deep. *The Kate* had been moored very high in the morning, so as to be dry enough to scrub in the afternoon; the water, however, left the boat for only a short time, but such interest was aroused that the fair sex defied the flowing tide, and hugged *The Kate* in spite of wet feet and stockings. Perhaps the greatest compliment I have received from any one was the fact of a fine old gentleman (one of the last century men) actually coming down to the pier, at a very early hour, to uncover his noble silver locks to the little boat as it departed on Monday, the 19th. There are no compliments like those that come from honoured age, and I was sorry to leave the place without finding out who the stranger was. He had spoken to me the day before, and I noticed that he took his whole family to view the tiny craft.

A tidal harbour always inflicts the loss of an hour or more of the tide, a very serious delay, leaving only 4½ hours in which the mariner has to work his boat some fifteen or twenty miles to the next harbour, as often as not in a dead calm. The wind was slap in my teeth, and fresh at first, though it died away to nothing. The distance to Trevose Head is about eight miles in a straight line. There is hardly any tide in the bay, so that a head-wind makes it a tedious cruise until the point is rounded. I kept a long way out to sea, so as to get as much tide as possible, because I found that I could not round the head before the tide turned against me; so that the best policy was to keep well out, and give the boat the chance of stemming the ebb.

Trevose Head is a very hazardous point, for the tide forms a very troublesome race as it passes the dangerous rocks called the " Quays." To round the head on the ebb with a light air is a dangerous experiment for one man, because the boat cannot be called in a safe position until in Padstow Harbour, from the simple fact that, should the wind drop altogether, the ebb might sweep the boat down upon the rocks. There is a first-rate roadstead east of Trevose and south of the Gull Rock, but an attempt to get there on the ebb, when becalmed, might end in going on the Quays instead; for the one hand can only work one oar effectually, and in all such positions, as a rule, the full strength of two men is wanted, for very few single men can last long enough to fight the battle out. I had no intention of going into Padstow, but made in-shore, so as to cheat the tide as much as possible; for the wind died away to next to nothing, being very fitful and light.

I was off Pentire Point, to the west of the Newland Rocks, when I became aware of the unpleasant fact that some strange set of the tide would not allow me to weather the rock. I spent some time in the attempt, and then gave it up as useless. There is a capital passage inside, but I did not like to attempt it, with the wind as it was, for the coast is a mass of rocks to the east of Pentire Point, and (what is the important point) the land stretches out to windward, Rump Point being to the north and east of Pentire, so that, becalmed on the ebb, I would have been put ashore to a certainty.

Listen to what the *Pilot Book* says about Padstow, page 3: "It is to be observed that the harbour of Padstow should never be attempted on an ebb tide or in stormy weather, unless you have a leading wind." The reason why the harbour is not to be attempted on the ebb is, that the tides race out of it six miles an hour at springs, and at least three at neaps. But it is a dangerous harbour to attempt, even on the flood, for the channel is excessively narrow, the whole space on the left-hand or east side being a dangerous sand, called the "Doom Bar." The winds also eddy from the heights, and utterly baffle the sails. My choice lay between anchoring outside, in about nine fathoms of water, on a sandy bottom, attempting the harbour, or the roadstead in Mother Ive's Bay, distant 3½ miles. The last alternative, being a backward move, was dismissed; to attempt the harbour was an excitement; to cast anchor was the very reverse; consequently, I determined for the harbour. The direction of the wind was about NW., hardly any at all.

To make Padstow, keep close to the rocks on the right-hand side. The *Pilot Book* and all my informants said the same thing, consequently I followed their advice; the oar, as a matter of course, was doing its part of the work, but under great difficulty. I do not suppose it is possible to make any but a sailor realise the motion of a lively boat in a tideway with a light air dead astern. Let me explain that a tideway is always more or less rough, that the water is travelling at a great pace, and knocks the boat about in the most wonderful manner, especially if it is going against or across the stream unsteadied by the breeze. The boat may be fairly said to go mad, in the little short jumbling bubble, which almost baffles description. The little pyramids of water are not strong enough to support anything, and their elevation and depression is excessively rapid. To have to row a boat in a fair sea tideway is bad enough, but in hollow, broken water the difficulty is increased by the rapid action of the boat. If the wind is light every difficulty is aggravated by the swing of the mainboom; a whack on the head, a rap on the knuckles, or the skinning of the upper hand may be expected at every stroke, by a playful movement of the boom, oar, or main-sheet.

I know nothing so calculated to annoy the unfortunate boatman as the action of the mainboom or sheet in a position of this sort. If the boom is lashed to one of the mainstays, and a turn of the sheet taken round some other belaying-pin, at an angle to its own, the nuisance is put an end to, and the single-handed oarsman may safely calculate on a few seconds' peace; at the end of which time he will most likely find that the sails are all aback, and that the boom and sheet must be allowed to play about as before. Every little action requires time, so that, when contending with a tide, it is much the best to let the sails look after themselves in positions where sudden eddy winds may be expected and rocks or sands are close by.

I rowed away as hard as I could, keeping quite close to the rocks (within a few yards), and thereby hit off an eddy tide, which helped me round the point, on which was a large board, with the words, "Keep this side." A puff or two of wind assisted me along now and then, but I was beginning to tire under the exertion, having only just held my own for at least twenty minutes after rounding the point, and was about to sheer off from the rocks (which I could almost touch with the oar), so as to put an anchor down, when, to my great delight, I saw a boat coming down at a great pace on the ebb, with but one man in it. The pilots at Padstow are always on the look-out. This man had seen me long before, but had not supposed I would attempt the harbour, and made for his boat, only on seeing *The Kate* appear unexpectedly round the corner. A rope was soon made fast, and what with his towing, my rowing, and a little assistance from the wind, which very kindly increased, *The Kate* arrived safely at an anchorage in what is called the harbour-cove, a very snug little place for small craft. The following summary may be an assistance to small craft attempting the capital anchorage mentioned above, on an ebb tide, with a fair wind and oars, without which latter assistance the effort must often fail:—

Keep out a little when the board has been passed, say forty yards from the rocks on the sand, where there is enough water at half-ebb for small craft, and the tide does not race so hard as in the correct channel. Make in towards the rocks again when close to the bar, which can be easily distinguished by its white water. It is impossible to mistake the cove on the right-hand, in which even large vessels may lie on the mud. The town of Padstow is a long way up the river, and any attempt to proceed beyond the cove would be very unadvisable in a stranger, for a dangerous sand extends nearly the whole way, leaving a narrow intricate channel.

The yacht of Mr. Burrows was anchored in the cove, the owner representing the last of England's real yachtsmen that I had the pleasure of meeting. I was up very early in the morning, about 2.30 A.M., and had all the sails set in readiness to catch the splendid breeze which was blowing from the SE. The pilot did not arrive till 4 A.M., which made me excessively angry; for I did not like to go away without paying the man his five shillings, nor did I relish losing my time. At last, in great disgust, I hailed another man, and was in the act of getting the anchor up, at 4 A.M., when the pilot came along-side. I was riding at anchor very near the rocks, so that it was a risk to get under weigh single-handed; for, if the boat happened to get on the wrong tack just as the anchor tripped, the rocks might have proved themselves harder than the wood-work, and have put a summary end to the voyage. The breeze deserted me when round Pentire Point; I therefore anchored in Quin Bay, to await the tide, for I had started on the ebb. Coasters have ridden out very heavy gales in Quin Bay, just to the east of the Mouls Rocks, which have the effect of breaking the sea; but care must be taken not to anchor directly between the island and the main, for the tide runs very strong through the narrow channel. Anchorage is not recommended in Quin Bay; but as gales have the peculiar habit of not asking leave of presence, it may be of service to some unfortunates to know what has been done. I had been riding to the ebb for about an hour, when a cat's-paw from the south-west purred a gentle invitation to the sails.

> The cable heard, and hummed a joyful note;
> The anchor answered, 'Coming, all afloat.'

I was again becalmed off Port Isaac for a couple of hours, and haze obscured the land, so that I could hardly catch the bear-ing of Tentagle Point. A light head-wind enabled me to beat off that very formidable headland, and then I was becalmed again for the third time. My position was getting uncommonly awkward—

> For time and tide maintained their certain course,
> The rocks were rugged and the ebb aforce.

I had hoped to make Lundy Island that evening, but the idea died away during the calm at Pentire Point.

There is not a single harbour between Padstow and Ilfracombe which can be attempted with any great hopes of success in a gale, or even a strong breeze from the land. Barnstaple is, I believe, the only one which affords shelter from the ground-sea; but it is a most difficult place to make under the most favourable circumstances, and always requires a pilot, as the bar is formed of gravel and coarse sand, and is perpetually shifting. I sail by myself, it is true; but I would not attempt any harbour with a gravel bar without the assistance of a pilot, or, what is exactly the same thing, being shown in by some other boat. The *Pilot Book* says, at page 10, after discussing the dangers of making Barnstaple: "*But if in desperate cases by night*, in thick stormy weather, those who are entirely unacquainted should, for the preservation of life, be constrained to run for the harbour, they have only to keep the lights in view, as before directed, until they approach the outer light to less than 200 fathoms distance." The difficulties appear to commence at the outer light, but there is no further necessity to inflict them on the reader, the extremity of the danger being clearly expressed in italics. The passage, however, is a good sample of the way in which difficulties are increased by the use of wrong words. It can only be a nuisance to have to discover the equivalent of 200 fathoms distance, even supposing the reader in an ice-box. It is much better to state the number of yards; and this remark will also apply to the expression, "a cable's length."

The oar had been at work nearly all the morning, being a matter of course in light airs. It was utterly useless to keep on in hopes of making Hartland Bay—but where was Boscastle? I had been warned that it was a blind place to find; but I could see no earthly trace of it anywhere, although I was at an offing of nearly two miles from Tentagle Head. The coast to Boscastle is peculiarly rocky, and I recognised it as forming the subject of a large painting I had seen at the hotel at New Quay. The rocks are, in fact, one of the sights of Cornwall, both from their peculiar structure and the fearful surf that breaks all around. I could see a small white substance among the rocks, and distant about three miles, but could not make out what it was, even with the assistance of the glasses. One thing, however, was very certain—I must make an anchorage before ebb time, or be compelled to return to Padstow. I therefore considered the matter over a pipe, and determined to hazard the chance of the white speck being a coaster off the entrance to Boscastle, and I was right. The risk of attempting to row in was by no means a small one, even to two men; for, supposing I had missed, I would have been at the mercy of the powerful ebb, which would have caught me utterly exhausted by the row in, and have swept me on the rocks, or compelled me to cast anchor in a very dangerous position, with the chance of the anchor cragging over the rocks. It must be remembered that the flood was carrying me rapidly to the north and east, and I had to row a distance of about two miles before the tide turned or swept me past the port. The latter no mean risk, for the very dangerous rocks called the " Beeny Sisters" are just on the other side, and the tide sets right on to them. In fact, the currents are very strong and irregular on both sides of the excessively disastrous harbour of Boscastle, and it would be a difficult matter to say which offers the least hazardous approach.

The sun was most distressingly hot, and there was not even the very slightest motion in the air to deflect its burning rays. The continued exposure to the sun, coupled with the constant drain on physical energy, had produced a burning thirst and a general state of feverishness which would have been fatal to the expedition but for the splendid constitution that nature has bestowed upon me. In fact, the row into Boscastle was very nearly being the last feather, and I doubt if any inferior organism could have got through it, starting, as I did, after a heavy morning's work and two or three weeks of continued toil beneath a blazing sky. I steered the boat so as to make an acute angle with the direction of the tide. A right angle would have been fatal. I hoisted my pilot jack before starting, so as to give myself every chance; for it would never do to have to stop at a critical moment to hoist it; and had I gone ashore without it up, the world would have had some slight pretext for a cry of "foolhardy." My row over the tide at Spithead was hard work, but it was at the commencement of the trip, when I was comparatively fresh, and it did not distress me after the manner of this particular one.

The entrance to Boscastle is hidden from view by a large rock, which stands exactly in front, and forms two narrow channels, one on each side, about twenty yards wide, which are completely rock-locked. The inlet winds towards the harbour for nearly 100 yards, and leaves little more than room for one coaster at a time. I should say, at a guess, it took me at least one hour and a half to row in; out of which, the half was nothing short of excessively severe punishment. So intense was the pulsation throughout my whole frame, that I thought something must go smash; and I shall never fear breaking a blood-vessel for the rest of my existence. The brain thumped against the skull as I hope never to feel it thump again; and it was some time after my anchor was down before I could congratulate myself on being quite sound. The pilots appeared, on a message being sent to them, and towed *The Kate* inside the inner harbour. I was given to understand that the boat was found and the pilots were paid by a lady named Miss Ann Avery Hellyar, who takes great interest in the shipping of the port, and provides for the ready assistance of strangers.

Boscastle may be considered one of the fashionable resorts of invalids and tourists, and it boasts a capital hotel, a long way in advance of many found in much more important places— in fact, it would be hard to meet a cleaner or better-appointed establishment. The landlady is very obliging and peculiarly suited to be the mistress of a first-class hotel. One of the very first questions the pilots asked me had reference to ropes. People have different ideas on most subjects, according to the corners of the earth in which they dwell, and according as they are stationary or the reverse. Had I any ropes? I certainly thought I had, and wondered at the question, as my cable was staring the inquisitors in the face. I answered, with a sort of honest pride in considering the craft well found, that I had two or three cables on board, which would hold *The Kate* in a gale, as long as they did not chafe. But the pilots only smiled, and said, "We will look after the craft for you, sir, and can lend you a rope or two if necessary." Had I sprung a leak in my brain-pan, after all? or what was the row with my cables, that they should meet with such contempt, and be actually smiled at, in a pitying sort of way, as if mere twine, and one the gallant cable I had ridden to over and over again, and let the heavy squalls do their worst? A giant hawser met my wondering gaze—"That is a rope," was the answer to my Query No. 1. No. 2 bringing the response, "For the ground-sea, sir." "Ground-sea!" I exclaimed, in intense astonishment; "pray how can it possibly get in?" "Oh, over the cliff sometimes, sir; but it comes in by the channel, and smashes everything to bits."

The cliff is only a hundred feet high, and the channel like a ram's horn. If there ever was a harbour in any world in which the wearied mariner might hope to rest securely for a while, such must have been Boscastle, or its second self. The port is so retired and completely land-locked, that at low-water the sea might be a thousand miles off: and yet there is not a more treacherous spot in the world. The ground-sea rushes in with the most amazing violence at dead low-water, and has been known to hurl vessels right up the bed of the river towards the village. Should the immense hawsers stand the first blow, the return shock will usually part them like packthread, when the vessels are very rapidly reduced to their first elements. The ground-sea is at its worst during the heavy winter gales; but its character is most eccentric. It will often run in a most violent manner on the calmest of all calm days, sometimes for hours, but as often as not for a short time, when, after smoothing down again, it will be raging mountains high in another half-hour. The cause of the ground-sea is a mystery; but science has cleared up a great many mysteries, and might do something

73

towards solving this problem. The causes, however, are peculiarly difficult to study, for they must be searched for while the sea is on; and one thing is certain, that no known vessel can live in it. I imagine that strong irregular currents setting in from the westward are in a great measure the cause of the sea, and that not only from their force, but from one of the primary causes of their motion, namely, temperature. I have seen the water near Padstow, to the north-east of the Newland Rocks, disturbed, and wearing the appearance of boiling springs rushing to the surface. Such would be local causes of derangement. The actual breaking of the sea is caused by the top currents overrunning the lower, which are impeded by the rugged bottom. This drag is greater or less in proportion to the nature of the bottom and the depth of water, which latter lessens or intensifies the action of gravitation, the shoaler water concentrating the combined action of these powers, and compelling the surface stream to form a huge overhanging wave, which breaks with immense violence from its own weight. Nothing can be done during continued gales; but patent log lines and thermometers might be laid down at different depths, and be examined, as often as possible between tide times, but especially after a partial commotion of an hour or so without apparent cause.

CHAPTER VIII

FROM BOSCASTLE TO MILFORD

I LEFT Boscastle on the 21st of July, at 5.30 A.M., bound for Lundy Island. The breeze was very fresh off the land, and came down in sharp squalls; the pilots advised me to keep quite close along the land, so as to cheat the tide. They were going to examine their fishing nets and lines just off the Beeny Sisters, consequently we sailed together that distance, and I kept close in-shore; but afterwards I steered out, in spite of the tide, for I found the winds eddy in the most perplexing manner, being at one moment south-east, and the next deflected by Sharp-nose Head and the line of cliff to about north-east, which was, of course, slap in my teeth. I lost at least two hours of a fine breeze by hugging the shore, but I learnt my little lesson, and have most carefully avoided the close neighbourhood of elevated lands ever since. I did not hold the true wind until I had gained an offing of at least $1\frac{1}{2}$ miles, shortly after which time the land breeze died away and a head-wind met me from the north. The tide had turned in my favour, on which I stood well out to sea, being some six or eight miles out, so as to catch the full tidal swing, and so as to be to windward of my course for Lundy Island: which was the main point. Had I hugged the shore, I never would have got there, for this simple reason, that the flood would have set me up the Bristol Channel, and the ebb out of it again; for I would have had to cross both those tides close-hauled, whereas, as it happened, I stemmed one of them towards the evening with a flowing sheet.

The head-wind lasted throughout the afternoon, and was very light. I became aware, every now and then, of a heavy swell, which lasted for a few minutes on each occasion and then died away, affording a very slight example of the eccentricity of the ground-sea, which was evidently commencing to run, and, as it happened, was the precursor of

75

heavy weather. I was in company with a number of ships, some apparently bound up the Bristol Channel, for they were hugging the land at a distance of only three or four miles; thirteen others were steering for Lundy Island, which could not be seen, because the weather was hazy. The wind had shifted to the dreaded north-west, and quickly knocked up a very nasty, disagreeable sea. The glass had been falling for some short time, and altogether the weather looked very threatening. First one ship made off, and then another; some of them running off, and then hauling up again, as if not quite certain of the best course to pursue. But one and all made away to the eastward, and *The Kate* was left alone in her glory.

It would be impossible to say how many times I peered into the thick atmospheric belt, which still continued to hide the island from my sight; it can be seen at a distance of twenty miles, if not more, and its lights, thirty. I knew that I was steering the proper course, that I was well to windward of the tide,* and that I must run ashore, if I only persisted; *ergo*, I did persist, and I saw the land, nearly three miles off, about 8 P.M., and the lights were visible very shortly afterwards. My bowsprit was pointing directly for the south-east corner— a very satisfactory land-fall, considering the boat's head had been in every conceivable direction for the greater part of the day.

I had discovered the want of port and starboard lights very early in the voyage, my very first night's trip from Brighton showing their importance. I therefore ordered a pair to be sent to me at Southampton, but it had not occurred to me to have the correct boards to lash against the rigging, for these lights to fit into and thus remain steady and serviceable. I had been content to use the riding light when out at night. The consequence might have been disastrous in the extreme. There is great danger of being run down off Lundy, because it marks the track of an immense trade; I therefore lit the side lights, and endeavoured to fasten them so that they might show their colours in the proper direction. All such attempts

* The fact was I had the tide so that I could stem it nicely with the wind at WSW.

turned out perfect failures, the most cunningly devised lashings having no other effect than to turn each lamp into a revolving light, the only change being when each lamp, in the most obstinate manner, turned its light on board, and there remained stationary. The only remaining light was then the white anchor light, and this also played about in a manner likely to damage it. I relit the side lights, but it was of no use— the very oil consumed the spring of life, impeded circulation, produced a stagnation in the lungs, which the doctor styled consumption. I thought that, if proper treatment was resorted to, they might exist; and, consequently, when arrived at Milford, I had a habitation made for each, the chimneys swept, the windows roomy, and arranged that ventilation might restore a healthy circulation, and support the rapid declination of the wick by a natural consumption of the oil.

There is much more in the correct handling of a side light than may appear at first sight, even to those whose peculiar duty it is to be learned in their many eccentricities. Such have often complained to me that it is no uncommon thing for a freshly-trimmed light to go out immediately it is placed in position, and that from no mechanical fault of the maker. I say, of the maker, because the dying of the lamp arises from the trimmer having made a mechanical blunder. It was very excusable that I should be guilty of a like error on a first acquaintance; and the very first time I lit my side lights, after having them properly mounted and ventilated, the starboard one most stubbornly refused to burn. A trial of side lights out of their places on board is as useful as observing a jockey on a rocking-horse. The reason will appear presently. I made my first trial in the daytime, so that I might have daylight to discover and correct any distressing peculiarity. There are many ways of doing some things, but only one best way. I always think the great charm of action lies in its tendency by the shortest and most certain lines.—"My starboard light will not burn"—such was reflection No. 1. No. 2 being, "But the port light burns." No. 3, "I am not aware of what is wrong; but (No. 4) I am certain that the wrong = the difference;" consequently, I took down the two lights and carefully examined

77

them both. Observing that the mechanism of each was the same, I struck that out of the equation, and the remainder was trimmer's mechanical wrong = difference; trimmer's mechanism = arrangement of oil and wick—*ergo*, the lamps must be differently trimmed. Had I forgotten to put any oil into the starboard one? The happy thought instantly created an action which showed that the lamp was very full of oil, for the slightest motion made the oil flow through a small hole in the wickholder. An equivalent tilt of the port light instantly produced the difference—the oil did not flow through its small hole. The mysterious action was cleared up; but why should the flow of oil put the light out? For the following simple reasons: that the jolt the overfilled lamp receives when being put in its place or from the motion of the vessel will cause the oil to extinguish the flame instantly; and, if placed with care, the water being smooth, the want of ventilation will cause a lingering death.

To return to Lundy Island and the progress of *The Kate*. I lit and lashed the riding light to the mizen-stay, and topped the mizen-boom so that the perfect crowd of vessels which were coming astern might not fail to perceive the little boat and direct their bows at a safe distance.

There has been one most remarkable feature in connection with my voyage; namely, that the wind has almost invariably failed me when attempting to make a harbour or an anchorage. It left me on this occasion within a half-mile of the roadstead; the night was dark, but I could hear the race-tide long before I struck it just off Shutter Point. Lundy Island may be said to form a mass of races, which are all dangerous at any time, from the fact that they may put a vessel ashore, but are excessively dangerous in heavy gales of wind, from the extraordinary seas which they create. The worst are the Hen and Chickens and the race of White Horses, on the north end of the island. The others are not of much account in fine weather, being simply disagreeable seas, such as the English Channel races. The great criterion of a race may be said to exist in the possibility or impossibility of an oar being worked. I am certain that no man living could have held an oar for one instant in the race off Peveril Point on the morning I passed through it; nor in the race of White Horses, or the sea on the St. Goven's Bank. I passed through the others on hot spring tides, recrossing that of the Land's End, in order to make the most of its velocity, as I was anxious to make Sennen Cove before the tide turned and a very light air prevented my rowing the boat head to wind. But I could have handled an oar (though to little purpose) in any of the races except those mentioned.

My white riding light seemed to attract the curiosity of large ships, for one steered straight at me, condescending a very slight deviation from its track on my singing out. The vessel in question was sailing towards the roadstead on the east of the island; but when I hailed, and asked the direction of the roads, a brutal laugh was all the answer I met with. I am sorry that the darkness prevented my reading the name, or I would have had the greatest pleasure in showing the vessel up. I was so close that the commonest conversation could be heard distinctly, and yet the humane officers on board had not even the sense or good feeling to answer, "Follow us, as we are going past." The vessel was a large one, and carried a number of quarter-deck officers, and, unless my eyesight deceived me very much, one commanded the forecastle who could only have been a pilot. Finding I must be out all night, I put the boat on its course for Milford Haven, and chose to pass to the westward of Lundy, to lessen the chance of being run down by the fleet astern.

The fresh favourable breeze was of short duration, and left me becalmed throughout the night to the westward of the north end of the island, in a very lumpy sea. It was so dark that I could form no notion of how to trim the sails—in fact, they could hardly be seen, and the mainboom, as usual, went about on its mad course. I made it fast once or twice, but found that I could not keep the boat's head in the right direction, and therefore had to loosen it again. To light a pipe and smoke by the light of the binnacle was of no use whatever as a guide for the distressingly light air, which was not enough to take the boat on, but was sufficient to baffle any attempt at steering in the tide, if the sails were taken aback. I therefore smoked away, and turned about until I found the smoke cutting my eyes from one and the same direction, and thus discovered the quarter from which the air was flowing—a guide I found of great service when cruising the north-east coast by night. I made some tea about midnight, on the principle of always being true to myself, for I could not tell at what moment my energies might be severely taxed. It is an odd thing that, although we often cannot eat, it is difficult to find any individual who is not always capable of drinking.

I will make no pretension to understand the tides by Lundy's isle; the fishermen I met informed me that it took them a whole year to make them out, and therefore my ignorance may be excused. The *Pilot Book* advances information, but I doubt its correctness. I enjoyed the night, the mere novelty of the position being an intense charm. I saw any amount of ships' lights from vessels lying becalmed, but at a considerable distance from *The Kate*. All that I could do was to watch the lights and take care not to be set ashore. The weather was so thick that I could not judge from the brilliancy of the lights if I was being carried back by the tide, for they would appear nearer or more remote in proportion to the thickness of the haze.

A dull roar from the rocks very soon put the question beyond doubt. *The Kate* was being drifted right upon the shore, the low light being no longer visible—a fact which spoke volumes. I fancy at that time (nearly 1 A.M.) I was not far from the Hen and Chickens Race.

> The paddle offered the resource,
> SW. the safest course.

It was terribly hard work rowing in the seaway and the dark. I forgot to count how many raps on the knuckles, scrapes from the mainsheet, whacks on the head from the boom, I received during the next hour, at the end of which time I became aware of a charming ounce breeze, just sufficient to do the work of the oar, allowing me to open both of Lundy's lights, to ruminate, create a third, to fumigate my thoughts.

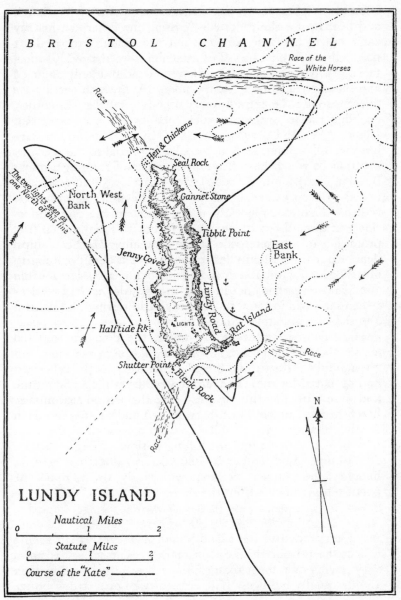

BRISTOL CHANNEL

Race of the
White Horses

Race

Hen & Chickens

Seal Rock

Gannet Stone

The two lights seen as
one North of this line

North West
Bank

Tibbit Point

East
Bank

Jenny Cove

Lundy Road

Halftide Rk.

2 LIGHTS

Rat Island

Race

Shutter Point

Black Rock

Race

N

LUNDY ISLAND

Nautical Miles
0   1   2

Statute Miles
0   1   2

Course of the "Kate" ———

81

I found myself at dawn just off the south point of the island, and beat up for the roadstead, passing the fishermen as they came out to lift their pots, but not near enough to speak. I passed through the race off Shutter Point for the second time, tacking across and across it, when the wind suddenly changed and blew a fresh strong breeze, about SW., which carried me safely through the extraordinary race-tide off the SE. corner, enabling me to anchor in safety about 5.30 A.M., with Rat Island SSW., and the farm-house W. by S. The salmon were jumping all around, seeming peculiarly partial to the race just mentioned, which has all the appearance of running straight through the island. I was sleepy and tired, but was compelled to keep awake, so as to catch the fishermen on their return, which took place about 9 A.M., when they came alongside, put a small boy on board, and went off to land their fish, promising to return at tide-time and anchor *The Kate* a good deal nearer in. I ate my last piece of bread, about one-fourth of a stale loaf, without a drop to drink of any sort. How would you like your gastric juice in such tip-top order as that, reader? I then sat down in the well, with my head resting on my arms and slept for a couple of hours.

The fishermen came at low-water, the boat was moored afresh, the sails made up, and I was glad to go ashore, about 3 P.M., and eat the capital breakfast the sisters of the fishermen had prepared for me. The family were from the Land's End, and were returning thither, this being the second season they had fished at Lundy. The fishery at the Land's End is too small for the number of its inhabitants, so that some of its members may be met at several of the fishing stations of Great Britain. A dashing, good-tempered idiosyncrasy, together with a haughty, independent bearing, will nearly always mark the poetic temperaments from the shores of Sennen Cove—

> The flashing eye, the honourable tread,
> Contentment's pluck adorn the weaker head.

A coaster traded to the island about once every ten days, to collect the fish for the London market. The fishery is not a very paying one, for it requires much more fine weather than Lundy usually indulges. The ground-swell or a strong breeze will often make the races impassable for fishing purposes; and the fish are frequently stolen from the pots, by a systematic course of pillage, on Sundays. I told the men I should try the effect of some small shot, as bringing the rascals up for thieving appeared no easy matter, there being a difficulty about powdering their heads, and a want of witnesses to the depredations. *The Kate* would have been piloted in safely enough but for these rascals, for the fishermen told me that they saw my riding light, but mistook me for a robber, and made off to their pots as fast as they could.

I was quite ready for breakfast, having lived on my loaf of bread the whole of the previous day. To say the truth, I preferred a wholesome piece of bread to the preserved meat, the former always appearing to me the most nourishing of the two. I doubt the necessity for the quantities of animal food devoured by the human race. Nothing proves the fallacy to my mind so much as the fact that whenever I go into strong work, such as rowing or canoeing, I invariably have to commence bread and beer, which I hardly ever touch at other times. I believe one meal a day of animal food to be ample for any man in good health, and fresh air; and that more is excessively heating and wastes the energies of life. I am of opinion that I never ate less in my life, in a given time of fourteen weeks, than I did during the cruise; and yet I recovered full health, extraordinary vigour, and weighed more at the end than I ever did before. Some people live chiefly by their lungs, others by their stomachs; and it would appear that nature has intended that there should be organisations fitted especially with such opposite tendencies. I am most certainly one of the lung order; a month in a town will reduce my vitality immensely, although I shall eat far more in the town than in the country. My large lungs delight in fresh air, and I am certain that they support and fatten to a great extent, though I cannot give a scientific reason for it, other than that they do their full share of work in fresh air, and either fall short of that work in city air, or else do it, but insist on compensation from other members. The point is one for medical men to discuss, but I presume that the power of nourishing the body is apportioned to its component parts—lungs, heart, liver, &c.—and that the power in each individual is *one and the same* with respect to that individual. If the above is true, it is easy to perceive that, if one organ fails in the slightest (as lungs must from want of fresh air), one of the other organs must make up the deficiency, the power remaining the same, so that, if we have less fresh air, we must eat more. This demand for more food arises, not only because the lung fails, but for another reason, which I wish to make conspicuous, that air itself is a nourishing body. I am not stating a novel fact, but I am endeavouring to throw more importance into an old one. I believe our huge cities to be a curse to the human race, though, of course, I can be answered at once, and be told that Manchester is not as large as London. I answer, Very true, but Manchester is big enough to contain all evils that arise from over-crowding; its peculiar ills arise from another reason, namely, its factories. But I recognise that the human race will do what it likes; I recognise its right to large cities, if it likes; but I also recognise another right, which belongs to me, namely, to remark that I think large cities a mistake.

This age is a great age. True; but it does not follow that every component part is great. There has always been a school which denies the right of speech, except under conditions which suit them—in fact, we hear that So-and-So has earned a right to speak; well, I believe I could write half a volume on the argument, but, to be Aristotelian, I will simply suppose that because A has held his peace for fifty years he must hold it for fifty-one, and because he has held it for fifty-one he must continue to fifty-two, and so on. There is evident wisdom in the cry of the babe. If it is necessary to walk in the presence of such, remember that a step to which a musician could play an accompaniment is of all things offensive. On such occasions, step off with a crotchet, then a quaver, a demisemi-quaver, a dotted quaver, a semi-quaver, a dotted crotchet, strike a piece of furniture, knock down the handsomest vase in the room, cut your nose nearly in two, and then open your ears. Six crotchets would have taken you out of the room, both in safety and peace, but, then, six crotchets would be dire offence.

84

It has occurred to my minute little brain that there is something very tell-taling in taking offence. Can the cap possibly fit? If a man struck me in the face, I suppose I might have some reason for being angry, but still I could not lose my temper without losing part of myself, even under those circumstances. If my temper is bad, the sooner I lose it and get another the better; but if it is good, I am evidently losing a good. If a man strike me, must I return the blow? I see no necessity! Christ says, "Turn to him the other cheek also." Why does A strike B? Because, in many cases, A is afraid of being called a coward, and for a like reason B strikes A; but if the accusation of being a coward was never heedlessly brought, A and B might both rise superior to the occasion. If such is correct, it is plain that A and B are naturally superior, but that man treads upon his nature.

The Cornish bread is decidedly the best that I have ever seen, and that which I tasted at Lundy Island would make the fortune of any baker, if it could be produced in the London market, instead of the bubbly, scentless, tasteless stuff which we are unfortunately condemned to eat. The loaves are usually large, and will fill a room with the fresh smell of corn; the grain is excessively close, but only of feather weight.

I have used the phrase "condemned to eat," and verily it means a great deal; I may also add "condemned to drink." It is no use having a penny, if you are compelled to put up with a halfpenny's worth; it is a dead loss of half your fortune —fifty per cent. deducted at once, and that in the most annoying way; for I would much rather pay fifty per cent. over, and obtain the article I want, than lose fifty per cent. the other way, the actual monied loss being the same in either case. Free trade is all very well, but free trade was never intended to spell "licence." It is plain that the capitalist with only a penny has no choice in the matter—he must pay his penny and get a halfpenny-worth; his is the cause which requires especial attention. The seller says, "If you can pay for my goods, you shall have them"; and he thinks that he is really stating the case honestly on its bearings. He says, "Do you want bread; I have loaves at one penny, twopence, threepence, of one and the same size and order of bread, but more attention is paid to the preparation of one sort than another, because we find it pays the trade."

To discuss the subject on its merits it is necessary to commence at the beginning; the radical idea must be exhumed for liberal discussion. What is the radical idea? Free trade? No; but trade is. Why is anyone allowed to trade? Oh, to make a fortune rapidly, or slowly, as the case may be, but certainly to make one as rapidly as possible. Such may be considered one radical idea about another radical idea; but is it the correct one? Certainly not.

Again I will ask, Why is a man allowed to trade? Why are the baker, the grocer, the butcher allowed to open their shops? Because the grocer must eat bread, the baker must eat groceries, and both baker and grocer must eat animal food. Life must go on; for once the creature is born, creation becomes responsible, and places its responsibility in the guardianship of certain of its parts. The stallion protects the troop of wild mares; the bull, the herd of wild cows; trees, hillocks, and rivers protect the grass and the cattle grazing on it. Take away the stallion, take away the bull, the trees, hillocks, and rivers, and the world would wither, parch, and die. A want is supplied to keep the stallion and his troop, the bull and his heard, the trees, hillocks, and rivers from preying on each other. Such a want is man; together with the other orders of creation. Man is born, and lives on the rest; generates acuteness, and makes bread. Savages become civilised, huts become houses, grass yields to cabbage, knowledge increases, collects the spice, and the grocer is made. Why is the baker made? Why is the grocer made? Because the rest of the world require the bread and the spice. Ages follow ages, houses become towns, towns become cities, shops are opened, licences procured. Why are licences procured—to raise money for the taxes? Partially so, but to throw a responsibility upon the seller. What responsibility? That of selling a sound article, and the soundest article for the money.

I have now arrived at an important point in the argument. I wish particularly to show that the seller is allowed to sell simply because others want; a certain responsibility is thrown on him, namely, to provide for a want. The carrying out his responsibility allows him to support himself, wife, and family; and as the making a certain amount of superfluous wealth cannot be guarded against, it is allowed. This is the second count that I wish particularly to point out; the trader is allowed to make money, but his doing so is not a recognised necessity, or a first cause of his being a trader at all. He is allowed to make money, as every one else is allowed to make money, but the State does not depend upon him individually for its wealth. It depends upon trade for its wealth, but not on the trader; to make myself better understood, I will say any particular class of trader. I am arguing the cause of the poor, and will stick to the baker. I have shown that he is allowed to open his shop because people want bread, and not because it is necessary to the State that he, the baker, should make a fortune.

And now I will pass on to the particular point of the discussion. Because *people want bread*, means a very great deal; a great deal more than the mere supplying the want. The poor man with his penny wants a pennyworth, wants fifty per cent. more than he gets, wants close-grained, corn-smelling bread, instead of bubbly, scentless, tasteless stuff. If the baker cannot supply it, take away his licence, and give it to one that will; to keep the one that will up to the mark, protect the poor man by appointing a public prosecutor, whose duty it shall be to examine the bread and prosecute the seller of bubbly, scentless, tasteless stuff.

"The least said, the soonest mended," is a very old saying. I could easily swell this book to a very great bulk if I chose. I could take the grocer and the butcher, in fact, half the world in turn, and I daresay I could find something fresh to say about each of them; but I do not see that the argument would gather force; if I did see it, I should not hesitate for a moment. I have pitched upon bakers simply because the poor have to live chiefly on bread; and I recognise that bread, such as the Cornish bread made by the Cornish women, is a real staff of life; but the bakers are not a bit worse than any one else.

The lights on Lundy Island are not well placed, being on the top, which is very often hidden by fog, while the foot can be distinctly seen. A gun should be fired every few minutes from the heights in foggy weather, and a new light erected lower down, so as to prevent large ships from mistaking the land for St. Ann's Head. The east roadstead at Lundy is serviceable as long as the wind is not easterly, but if it blows from that quarter, or looks threatening, vessels must depart elsewhere, the usual move being to the west side of the island, to Jenny Cove.

The day had been very dirty, with a strong westerly breeze, but the sky wore a very threatening aspect from the east, consequently I engaged one of the men to accompany me round, if the wind should change to the east during the night. It would have been the height of folly for me to attempt finding Jenny Cove in the dark, or even in the daytime, for that matter; for I do not think there is anything to mark it, and nothing in the world requires such care as the choosing an anchorage. The wind did not shift. I therefore set sail for Milford Haven about 4 A.M. I was advised to keep quite close in-shore, so as to avoid the race; I did so until off Tibbit Point, where the wind eddied in such a disgusting manner that I kept out and was carried through the race of White Horses; a decidedly dangerous race and a most fatiguing one, being three miles long. I struck it about the south-east corner and came out at the north-west one, receiving the full benefit of the distance. The tide swept me right off the north end of the island, where I both heard and saw the Hen and Chickens Race running like mad; and I verily believe that if the wind had dropped a little I would have journeyed through that also.

It is no easy matter to get out of the influence of the tides off Lundy, as they run four and five knots an hour. I made a great allowance for tide when crossing the Bristol Channel, which proved to be a very great mistake, because the tides run in different directions in different parts of the distance, and do not assist much, but if mismanaged are sure to cause great delay. The bearing course is the proper one to steer; a very smart sailing-vessel or steamer may be better navigated

by a slight compass allowance, if crossing just at the change of
tide, but a small boat with a strong breeze can hardly make
Milford in one tide.

I found myself about 3 p.m. in a very heavy sea, the heaviest
I had encountered anywhere. I sighted a good sized coaster
just as I was getting out of the worst of it, and therefore hauled
up quite close and asked the bearing for Milford. The man
who was lolling at the helm looked at me in a stupid sort of
way, as I was rapidly drifting out of hearing, and then coolly
said, "Have you no compass?" If there is one thing calculated
to annoy a man in want of information, it is to have a question
met by an idiotic query. I was so angry that I fairly roared
back the question, which had the effect of waking the individual, when he gave me the very best directions. The truth
of the matter was, the tremendous sea completely prevented
my determining the headlands, for I could only catch a
momentary glimpse as *The Kate* mounted a wave, my position
being something like that of the Trojans:

> Tollimur in cœlum curvato gurgite; et idem
> Subducta ad manes imos descendimus unda.
> *Æn.* iii. 564.

My friend, however, made one remark, which I take the
liberty of questioning. He told me to haul up NNW., because
the ebb was making down. The course was right enough, but
I cannot help thinking that it was a bastard ebb—in fact, the
flood running the wrong way—as is the case between Milford
and St. Goven's, where it makes to the eastward. He told me
the tide would turn at 5.30, which seemed correct enough;
but I am convinced that I sailed from St. Ann's to Milford
against a strong ebb, which detained me till midnight; and
this is borne out by the tide book, which gives 6.24 A.M. as the
time of high water on July 24. No amalgamation of tides
could have been more puzzling; I left Lundy about half-
flood, at 4 A.M.; 5.5 A.M. marking high-water at Milford on the
same day. I confess I give it up. All I know is, that some tide
or other kept sweeping me west as late as 9 A.M., and that I
steered against it, thereby making a mess of the whole affair,
for I ought never to have been near the St. Goven's Bank, had

I steered north-three-quarter-west, and allowed the tide to take the boat as far west as it could. The return ebb would then have set me up to St. Ann's about midday, and I would have got to Milford on the next flood. As it was, the ebb put me on the banks and into the bastard ebb, or inverted flood, which also placed me in a very dangerous position on the lee shore between Flinston and Linney Heads. I do not know a more dangerous iron-bound coast; the tide sets slap on to it, with a wonderful sea. There was just wind enough to let me beat off outside the Crow beacon.

A heavy squall struck me when off Flinston. It would have been madness to run the boat off towards the lee shore; I therefore let go the peak, lowered the main halyards a foot, and kept on my course. Happily it was only a squall, or *The Kate* would not have been heard of any more. The coast line to the immediate east of Linney is very badly marked in the charts; the minor headlands are not properly defined, and Freshwater Bay is too deeply indented, giving the idea of great depth, which it does not possess. The indraught to the east of Linney Head is very great; I tacked a quarter of a mile to windward of a pilot boat, with which I had been holding my own, but I was greatly astonished to see it suddenly to windward and ahead, although I knew it was not sailing faster than I was. I had tacked towards the beacon, and quickly discovered a tremendous tide running directly in his wake; I therefore took the hint, tacked again after the pilot boat, and, drifting nearly as fast, I soon weathered the beacon, and made rapid progress over the racing tide and heavy sea towards St. Ann's Head, about 6.30 P.M.

The entrance to Milford Haven is badly laid down on the chart, and the course dangerously described in the *Pilot Book*. Both mention Stack Fort as if the only fort, and neither takes the smallest notice of its colour, which is gray, a point that should be most carefully noted. There is a fort on Thorn Island, which has a dark ground; but any stranger coming in at night might easily mistake it for the Stack. Again, the position of Angle Bay is very badly marked on the chart; I can perfectly understand a stranger, running in at night, mistaking

Thorn Island for the Stack, its bay for Angel Bay, and becoming a perfect wreck. It was very dusk when I arrived opposite Thorn Island; and had I paid any attention to the directions in the *Pilot Book*, I would have passed on the wrong side of Thorn Island, mistaking that for Stack Fort, which I could not see. I had learnt to depend entirely on my own judgment very early in life, and carried the principle to the cruise; I therefore closed the *Pilot Book* in disgust, and chose my own course, rounding the channel buoys as well as if in broad daylight. To show how dark it was, I stood still without gaining a yard for about one hour exactly opposite the Stack, and yet it was not till next morning that I made out what the gray-coloured lump actually was. The night was bitterly cold, and the temptation to anchor very great, but I determined to keep on, and threw down the kedge off Milford at twelve midnight.

I was astir again shortly after 3 A.M., got the anchor up and sailed close in, hunting for a more convenient anchorage, but had to sail out again, as I could not find sufficient water to let me be sure that the boat would remain afloat. I passed the 24th in reading, answering letters, and writing up my log, intending to start for Wexford on Monday morning, if the weather was suitable.

My glass fell very suddenly on Saturday afternoon, and a heavy blow followed on Sunday morning from the westward. The glass continued to fall, and a strong gale blew throughout the night, which flew to NNW. on Monday morning, but backed to W. in the middle of the day.

At Milford I took the opportunity to see to all my lights, and in addition to the side lights, which have already been noticed, I found that my cabin lamp required putting in order. This lamp had been constructed with an awful spring, such that when attempting to fix the candle down with the cap, it was found to be exceedingly difficult to keep the spring down, sufficiently so as to allow of the cap being screwed on! The untoward force of this spring had led to several mishaps, in that both candle and cap had been repeatedly shot overboard —and here at Milford, it was necessary to have a fresh cap made. One of the pilots procured this for me, but on his attempting to fix it, the spring took charge once more, and hurled both cap and candle away again, and just missed striking him an awkward blow in the face! That was a spring —and it got the better of all of us, and I had to do without my cabin candle in consequence.

The tide flows to the north at St. Ann's Head at half-flood, and consequently it is against all the way from Milford, which rendered it necessary for me to drop down to Dale Roads, so as to be able to get away on the first of the flood from St. Ann's.

It was necessary to settle my account at the hotel—the "Lord Nelson," if memory serves me right—amid the crowd of those establishments I have visited lately. The landlord was out, but I tendered a cheque to the mistress, who quietly refused to take it. I had quite enough money to pay with, and I told her so; but it was a nuisance to part with ready-money for such a purpose, in a part of the world where there might be a difficulty of renewing that description of ballast. I was therefore rather irate at my cheque being refused; moreover, I happen to consider a doubt an insult, an unfortunate way of looking at things in the present day; but still an idiosyncrasy I shall hope to carry with me to the grave. I was quite determined I would not pay except by cheque; and when the landlord returned I performed my first feat in oratory. He had excellent reasons for his refusal; but I am happy to say that they one and all vanished before the indignant warmth I poured upon the scurvy rogues who had cast a slur upon the honourable title of gentleman. The landlord had one law-suit on hand to recover, and several others pending.

CHAPTER IX

FROM MILFORD TO KINGSTOWN

I LEFT Milford about 9 A.M. on Tuesday the 27th for Dale Roads, four miles away, with a light head-wind nearly due west. On the way down, I encountered some sea-going barges, and did very well with them, and received a very especial compliment from one of the bargees. The correct anchorage in Dale Roads is opposite a very old ruin on the left-hand side, which is so small that I entirely failed to make it out, and brought up opposite a broken tower to the north, which gave me the trouble of shifting my position after going ashore in the dingy. I was all ready to start at 4 A.M. on Wednesday, but a calm delayed me till 7.30 A.M., when, having lost three hours' flood, a light air SE. enticed me to lift the anchor; but I had to cast it again, as the wind was not sufficient to enable *The Kate* to work to windward over the flood. The breeze was SW at ten o'clock, a dead calm being reported off St. Ann's Head by the telegraph man at 11 A.M. Such had been the weather more or less since Monday morning.

I dined at 3 P.M. at a little Welsh inn, walked to the heights, and surveyed the islands. The Smalls' light was very distinctly visible; an infallible sign of bad weather, which I quickly found verified. I gained the deck at 5.50 A.M. on Thursday the 29th, and found an invitation to breakfast pinned on my fore-rigging. A light air from the SW. disturbed my flag, consequently the invitation was left to be answered from Ireland, and *The Kate* got under weigh, and made St. Ann's Head, after a tedious beat to windward. The wind, which was deflected SW. in Dale Roads, was about W. by N. outside—not very promising for a trip to Ireland, so as to hit off the passage through the banks opposite Wexford, the course being NNW., northerly from the Bishop's light.

The glass was very low and the weather threatening. The pilots were hove-to off St. Ann's Head, but on seeing me they very kindly stood across, and gave me a hint to put back, as the wind was not in a very favourable direction, and a coming storm was very plainly to be seen. However, I thought I would be able to manage somehow; and to put back for what might only be a shower, after all, was not to my taste; in fact, I had not once put back to a port I had left, and determined I would take my chance of making some other place, though I had not the vaguest notion where to look for a haven. That was just the point I could not gain satisfactory information about, as no one seemed to be learned in the geography of St. Bride's Bay. I was advised to pass through Broad sound, as being the shortest cut and offering the smoothest water, but when surveying these channels and islands from the cliffs I had made up my mind to pass outside of all if I possibly could, and therefore hauled close to the wind. But I soon found that the tide would make a very doubtful matter of my weathering Skokholm and the wind was rapidly freshening and at last blew quite a fresh gale; the helm was therefore put up for Jack Sound, a very narrow passage, which is more dreaded by the seamen than any on that peculiarly dangerous coast. A large rock called the Blackstone stands in the centre; a reef of rocks runs nearly across to it from Skomer Island, and a strong racetide converts the whole place into a mass of broken water; so that the most skilful eye would be perfectly thrown out in an attempt to judge the whereabouts of the rocks. I had not the smallest notion on which side I was to pass the Blackstone; I therefore put on my lifebelt for the second time during the trip, so as to have a chance if the boat struck. The gale had burst in the meantime, and drove *The Kate* at a great pace through the surging tide.

I hove-to under the lee of Skomer Island, double-reefed the mainsail, ruled off the course for Gouldtrop Roads, and ran. I had drifted to the Garland Stone, and was making from that point when I saw a fishing-boat beneath the sheltered lee. I felt quite certain it had some refuge close by; I therefore hauled to the wind just opposite the North Haven in Skomer Island, took the fishing-boat in tow, and was steered in by one of the men. The boat astern was much larger than *The Kate* and had to be cast off just at the entrance and rowed in, because the boards to windward were so short, the puffs so heavy, and their direction so uncertain, that it required a very handy craft to work in at all. The creek is a small indentation, about eighty yards deep and fifty wide; the east side has a dangerous reef of sunken rocks, which makes the entrance difficult for a stranger to attempt; but the holding-ground is first-rate, and has saved large brigs in heavy gales from the NW. Those vessels were shown it by the proprietor of the island, Mr. Vaughan Davies, who was kindly enduring the drenching rain and cutting wind in the attempt to serve me a like good turn; but I did not see him, being occupied with sails and charts. He came off to *The Kate* when at anchor, took the crew away in his gig; sheltered and refreshed the inner man. The gale increased towards 12 A.M., reducing a large vessel to a close-reefed maintopsail, and compelling it to beat backwards and forwards under the lee of the island throughout the whole day. It must have envied the position of *The Kate* in the snug little creek, but the wind would have rendered it a very hazardous experiment for a three-master to attempt an entrance.

There is not a safer place in the world for a small craft to be caught in than St. Bride's Bay; but if the unfortunate skipper does not know his ground, and loses his head, there is not a more dangerous spot. The south side contains North Haven, Martin Haven, St. Bride's Haven, Mill Haven, and Gouldtrop Roads, all of which shelter from winds, to the southward of east and west, while Ramsay Sound offers a splendid roadstead, let the wind be from any quarter. The best anchorage in Ramsay is opposite a white house, which I was given to understand could not be mistaken. The *Pilot Book* gives a dreadful account of the place, but I got my information from men who were well acquainted, and told me they would rather be at anchor in Ramsay Sound than any place in the bay, for the simple reasons that riding is as secure there as elsewhere, while the vessel can always get to sea from one end or the other.

The north side of St. Bride's Bay offers a capital anchorage in Solfach Roads, but a small craft will find South Haven, in Skomer Island, afford the best anchorage in a northerly gale. It is a very small creek, lies just to the west and south of Jack

Sound, and, should it be full, Milford is pretty handy. Skokholm does not contain a single legitimate anchorage of any sort, and is surrounded by dangerously strong tides. Vessels are frequently put ashore on these islands by the tides, when becalmed; so that coasters in the vicinity of Milford should be especially well found in riding gear.

I was puzzled when entering the North Haven by a vast number of minute white spots, which shone against the cliff and glistened on the edge, like large eggs carefully arranged in most military order. A closer survey showed a line of dark bodies, which lined the cliff in a most determined attitude, ready to defeat any antagonist by a gravity of importance which could not fail to impress the feeling of intrusion; while the very quiet reception instantly crushed all hopes of storming such a fortress. These pugnacious, pompous, stupid, selfish, brutally-quarrelsome, dirty little birds command the whole cliff above the North and South Havens; the guillemots, oyster-catchers, kittiwake gulls, &c., being more sociable, inhabit the southwest corner, the famous headland called the Wick, where I had the pleasure of seeing them in countless thousands, when I was accompanying my host, hostess, and guests in an evening ramble through the heather. The Wick forms a deep gully between a precipitous headland and an enormous ledge, presenting a fine sight as the billows surge against the cliff, rebounding in a pallid fury to the deep. The island affords good seal fishing, splendid woodcock shooting, and swarms with rabbits as it would with grouse; but the sea-birds do an immense amount of mischief, and are rapidly thinning the bunnies—in fact, destroying the property of Mr. Davies without affording him the smallest compensation.

A law has been passed lately to preserve the sea-birds. It is argued that they are of great use in warning the mariner off rocky coasts in tempestuous weather. The habit of the birds in such weather is to confine their flights to short distances, preferring to wheel them over the land itself. Few vessels would stand a chance of escaping the rocks in an on-shore gale, if once within sound of the cry of a kittiwake gull. Again, it is argued that the birds are being exterminated, because fewer than usual flock to our shores. This argument is not sound without its complement, namely, that the total number of sea-birds is lessened throughout the world. It is possible that, like human beings, they may relish new habitations, especially as they see themselves adorning our bachelor-full-stops. On exposed cliffs and islands, such as Skomer, the eggs of the birds form an excellent provision for the table. A trade in their skins allows the fishermen to procure the necessaries of life. A law depriving these men of their daily means of subsistence is just as hard as any other law would be that deprived any other community of its daily means of subsistence. Granting that a law is necessary for the general preservation of sea-birds, care should be taken that it is not a direct oppression. The action of the law in Skomer Island appears a direct oppression, as rabbits, domestic poultry, and game stand no chance, unless protected against the birds. To allow a puffin advance on a country wanted for the means of supporting civilised human life, is analogous in point of utility to suffering a tribe of Red-skins to regain the United States. It is a mistake to suppose the birds only live in the cliffs; they make holes just as far inland as they dare, consequently a territorial warfare is necessary at Skomer to keep them from overrunning the whole island, and such warfare can only be carried on in the breeding season, for the birds are gone by October. Again, they are useless at Skomer, for vessels cannot approach that island without passing a number of other marks, such as the Smalls' light, Grassholm, and Shokham, together with the Bishop's lights to the north; *ergo*, the preservation of the birds on Skomer evidently lessens their number on places like Flamborough Head, where they are supposed to be useful.

I was glad to accept my host's kind offer of a bed, as it allowed my wet clothes to be dried in the first instance, and have a chance of remaining so, for, as things turned out, every second that I could keep dry was a very decided advantage. Mr. Davies put me on board *The Kate* in the morning, about 6.30 A.M. The weather had moderated, but the glass still remained very low. The wind was about west, and light; but I had a reef in each sail, because I felt certain of more wind, from the state of the glass and the westerly quarter. Winds have peculiar characters, according to their localities. The west wind, on a westerly coast, usually increases in force as the day advances, dying away again gradually towards sunset.

The flood began to make up about 7 A.M., at which time I was under weigh for Ireland. I steered about north-west; but the tide set me down so fast to the north that I weathered the Bishop light by a bare mile only, at 10 A.M. The racing sea off the Bishops was very heavy; however, I hove-to, shook out the reefs, and had barely done so before I had every inch that I could carry, the puffs coming from the north of west. I put the boat on her proper course for Wexford; not that I wished to make that harbour, but in hopes of sighting the Tuskar light, thus hitting off the channel through the banks, when I could run along the land or anchor anywhere I saw vessels brought up. The thick weather put a complete stop to that arrangement, as I could not see the Tuskar, although it is visible ten miles off; nor could the coast line be distinguished, except when nearly ashore.

I was not quite certain, on leaving London, whether I would sail *viâ* Ireland or the Isle of Man. I bought a chart of the latter, thinking there might be some difficulty in buying it elsewhere; but feeling confident I could procure those for Ireland at Milford, if the necessity should arise. In this I was grievously disappointed, and had to chance the passage with no better guide than an old three-channel chart I purchased at New Quay, an utterly useless article for my purpose; the Government sheets, or others on a similar scale, being necessary to enable a stranger to navigate the banks which render the east coast of Ireland, as far as Dublin, so excessively fatal to shipping. The tides run across these banks at four knots an hour, and the sea breaks upon them in a most dangerous manner whenever it is blowing hard.

The expression "the sea breaks" will convey little or no meaning to many; but it means, that if a vessel is obliged to tack, and is struck when head to wind by one of the above-mentioned seas, it may go down stern foremost, drowning every one on board. If struck on the stern when running, the unfortunates on deck will most likely be drowned, the vessel be thrown head to sea, to be finished by the next one. Should the vessel touch the bottom, she will be a perfect wreck in three minutes, if not sooner. I passed two vessels off the Bishops, which were sailing close-hauled. The wind was very hard at 12 P.M., compelling me to heave-to and reef. I ran on with one reef throughout till 5 P.M., when I hove-to again and double-reefed the mainsail. The gale on the previous day had made a heavy sea, which the strong breeze increased, both being on the port beam. I saw no other vessels from 11 A.M. to 3 P.M., during which time the crested breaking seas formed a magnificent panorama on every side, as far as eyes could pierce the misty gloom.

I was drenched every few minutes by the crest of some wave which flew right over the mast, making it bitterly cold work in the cutting wind. If any one wishes to form an idea of what I went through on that occasion, let him sit on an exposed beach in a strong breeze, and have a bucket of water poured down his back every ten minutes for six hours, after which he may sit where he is till nine at night, or indulge a yard each way as exercise ground, with nothing more to eat or drink than I had. There was considerable danger in a sea breaking into the well, as it might have washed me overboard; however, only one succeeded in topping the coamings, their height luckily keeping out all such as struck abeam.

I had taken the precaution at Milford to have a duck cooked, which had kept very well in the stern locker. I saw no reason why I should not eat, even if I could not drink: a little careful manœuvring produced the duck, which I commenced to gnaw, having only my left hand for the performance of carving, the right being strictly engaged with the tiller. There was no seasoning required, for the dashing spray gave a double zest to the feast by increasing my appetite and salting the provisions. I was nearly succumbing to the cold at 3 P.M., heaving-to, and drinking a glass of sherry; but I sighted a vessel heading my way, and thought it wise to do all I could to catch up and speak, as the weather had upset all my little arrangements. The boat was travelling very fast; for I was carrying a great deal of canvas in proportion to the strength of the breeze, so much so that on one occasion the boat seemed fairly in the air; from either having overrun the sea, or having been struck under the quarter. Whichever it was, she pitched right on the starboard bow, and went on as if nothing had happened. I was carrying as much canvas in the seaway, with the wind right abeam, as in the smooth water to Courtown with the wind right aft; and I rapidly caught the ship ahead. It stood across my bows, to my intense disgust, when another twenty minutes would have taken me alongside. A slight clearance of the fog showed some half dozen vessels manœuvring in the same manner. I therefore knew that a harbour was not far distant, and that the big ships dare not cross the banks. The change into comparatively smooth water also told me I was nearing land, so I determined to keep straight on, expecting to find myself in a bank-sea every minute.

A heavy squall at 5 P.M. compelled me to heave-to again and double-reef the mainsail. I therefore indulged in a glass of sherry; my first drop of anything to drink since the coffee at 6 A.M. I had unfortunately broken my flask, and determined not to replace it, so as to economise the excellent sherry Messrs. Hamilton and Grieve had furnished. It was kept in two four-gallon casks on the port side, beneath the main-hatch, so that in a heavy seaway it was absolutely necessary to heave-to before the golden drops could twinkle in the sun, or gild the pallid moon. I made the Lucifer Shoal lightship at 6 P.M. and was greatly put out by the sight of it, because I could find no mention of it in the *Pilot Book*, or the old-fashioned three-channel chart.

I have noticed the clumsy way in which pilot books are put together; here is another case in point. I discovered on October 27, 1869, that this lightship *is* mentioned in the addenda, most stupidly stuck in the middle of the work, accompanied by a polite request to the reader to transfer the alterations to their respective pages with the pen. Pray why were they not printed in their proper place? I presume a man is to lose his life to save trouble and expense to compilers of works, whose penmanship is bought expressly as a protection from danger.

Not being able to find any mention of this lightship, I

promptly determined to go alongside, and even now I am astonished at my audacity and skill in doing so under the circumstances!

The lightship struck me as being much larger than the ordinary run of those vessels—and it was rolling and plunging in the seaway—nevertheless I took her about amidships and, when some nice shooting distance off, I suddenly rounded to and put *The Kate* alongside with all the skill of a practised professional, and without a scrape or injury to my boat of any kind! In this I must confess that I was promptly met by as remarkable readiness on the part of Commander Dennis Murphy, who had some immense fenders over the side in an instant, and one or two of his hands jumped aboard my craft. I then learned that I was just off Wexford and had made an excellent course but Commander Dennis Murphy cautioned me against attempting that harbour, as it is said to be so dangerous to approach in dirty weather that even its own fishermen will not make the attempt.

I therefore tried to lay astern of the lightship, thinking it useless to proceed in such weather without a chart to show the way. However, the wind blew *The Kate* over the strong tide beneath the big one's stern and it was just touch and go that the mast was not whipped out of her. The foresail was then hoisted to windward, and this made her sheer off, but she did not seem inclined to lay like that without constant watching and the consequence was that I determined to proceed. On this the captain offered me a pilot, one of his men having volunteered to take the boat to Courtown. We left the lightship about 6.30 with two reefs in the mainsail, one of which was shaken out, but not hoisted for some little time, on account of an immediate fresh of wind. The pilot just skirted the Blackwater Bank, and made straight in-shore, when we ran close along the beach, heading out now and then for a reef or two. The flood turned with us just before we arrived at Ballyvalden Gap, where the pilot asked me to time the boat into Courtown. We passed the gap at eight, and the anchor had been down about five minutes when the pilot reminded me of the time, which was exactly 9.15 P.M., giving seventy minutes for the run from the gap, a distance of about twelve miles, and making the run from the lightship in about two hours and a half, the whole distance being 24 miles. I may as well add that both the pilot and myself were astonished at the manner in which she *spoke* to the nice-sized helpful seas going with her.

There are some very dangerous piles off Courtown Harbour, to look out for which I went forward into the bow; but it was so excessively dark that we were as near as possible on them, my cry of hard-a-port being only just in time. The said piles have wrecked many a Courtown fishing-boat; their detached nature renders it a difficult matter to keep a light burning protected in any ordinary way, for such require a great deal of trimming. My riding light was put up every night while *The Kate* lay in the harbour, and quite won the affections of the old watchman, who considered it exactly the sort wanted for the piles at winter time. I was therefore asked for the address of the maker, and a candle as a pattern; but the utter simplicity of the lamp was too much for one individual, who asked me, "Was I sure there was no oil wanted?" The beauty of the lamp consists in the fact that it requires no trimming whatever, and will burn for eight hours if the spring is kept clean, greased occasionally, and the lamp hung so that the candle retains a vertical line. The latter arrangement was impossible when I was sailing or riding in an open roadstead, for the motion swung the lamp about in a wonderful manner, the candle never being vertical for a second, the constant motion being the cause of its final disaster when *The Kate* was riding it out in the mouth of the Thames.

The fishermen at Courtown are of the generous, dashing order; and wherever they are known throughout Great Britain, they are noted for a generous, manly courtesy to the stranger.

The Kate was towed into Courtown Harbour about 9.20 P.M., and I was glad to get into bed, having suffered from a constant shower-bath from 11 A.M. till 5 P.M., and having sat in my wet things till near ten at night. The boat had made very little water, in spite of the tons which had swept over the decks, but the apparently trifling leaks, which have already been noted, completely wet most of the things through; though the damp atmosphere had just as bad an effect, and covered the inside of the boat with a beady perspiration in a very short time, rendering the rest of my clothes utterly unwearable. The main-hatch would keep out every drop of rain, but was excessively well ventilated on every side; even when shut close up, the draught in a strong breeze would then cause the candle to have an attack of the trembles, and would pour in such an amount of damp air that, even in my first few days out of London, I learnt the folly of buying more than one box of matches at a time, and the wisdom of having such made of wax. Cigar-lights of any description that I have tried are useless after an hour or two in damp weather; in fact, I would not trust them in any weather, as salt air always has more or less moisture in it, and the dry days are often accompanied by a heavy dew, which will utterly ruin both cigar-lights and wooden boxes of matches exposed to its influence. I was obliged to buy a new box of wax matches every day when on the Irish and Scotch coasts, or run the risk of not being able to enjoy a pipe. I found the wax matches kept dry for the greatest length of time in the small tray beneath the binnacle; but even with that protection they could not be depended upon after a few hours. I imagine the waistcoat pocket is the best place to keep a match in, for the heat of the body will guard it from the damp; but that resource was denied me, because a constant vapour bath, from labour at the oar or dashing spray, produced the necessity for some wringing agonies in the above-mentioned article. It would be a great boon if some one invented a match impervious to damp, and which would strike on a dry or wet surface, for on board a small boat the striker is often as much if not more to blame than the matches themselves. I have frequently lit the binnacle in the early daytime, and kept it burning, so as to make certain of having a light, but even that would often blow out in a strong breeze if the door was opened. Many dozens of the very best wax matches have been uselessly burned in an endeavour to light a pipe, the draught at the binnacle door putting the match out instantly, and necessitating the boat being brought to the wind at the great risk of a ducking.

I left Courtown at six o'clock on Monday morning, August 2, with a fresh breeze about WNW. It is hardly possible to make the distance to Dublin Bay with the wind in that quarter, as it is sure to draw ahead off Wicklow, and continue so as far as Dalkey Island, where it may fly all round the compass in a very short time. Wicklow Head is a nasty place for a stranger to be off in any weather, because it has a number of dangerous shallow rocky banks in its immediate neighbourhood. The Horse-shoe Bank was my particular enemy. The *Pilot Book*, at page 44, says:—"The Horse-shoe Bank begins at Wicklow Head, about half a cable's length from the shore, and extends SSW. along the land above a mile. The shallowest part is about half-way between the south end and Wicklow Head, where the least water is two feet, rocky; on the other parts there are from nine to three fathoms; between the shoal part and the land are ten feet. A black conical buoy is placed near the SE. edge of this bank in 4½ fathoms, with Wicklow lower lighthouse N. by E., and Mizen Head SW. ½ W. To sail without the Horse-shoe, keep Bray Head well open of Wicklow Head. To sail between it and the shore, you must keep a cable's length from the latter, until you are near the extremity of the head, then within half a cable's length until you have passed it."

I kept well out, although I had been advised to keep quite close in, to avoid the race. I saw a large number of small coasters taking the course inside, but I thought it hazardous, and just calculated the race at its full weight: in fact, I saw nothing but a nasty cross sea, which a strong breeze will always knock up in a four-knot tide. I held on till off Bray Head, where the squalls came down with such terrific violence that the water looked just as if blown out of a gun. The squalls off mountainous land give no warning; they strike the sails first, and are thus peculiarly dangerous. It was useless to keep on for Kingstown with a head-wind and a tide which was nearly done; I therefore put my helm up and made Wicklow.

The Irish and Scotch harbours which I saw resemble narrow streets more than anything else, being simply the mouths of small rivers, suitable for vessels of a small draught of water, which are usually towed in and out by tug-steamers or boats ahead. They are very awkward for small boats, which have usually to lash alongside of some coaster, the only way ashore being over its decks. A pilot is always necessary, for supposing the wind and tide favourable, a stranger cannot tell where he will be in the way or out of it, nor can he know the proper vessel to lay alongside of. Numbers will be going out the next tide, but it does not follow that they will say so, and he may find himself cast off at a moment's notice. However, as I said before, no man has a right to enter harbours by himself at the risk of damaging the property of others. I did so on the Scotch side because I could not get a pilot, but on one such occasion I had to be very thankful that my rigging was made of wire.

I went up into the town and dined at the best hotel I could see, slept on board, as a matter of course, and started for Kingstown on Tuesday morning, with the wind SW., but perpetually shifting for the first hour; the next thing to a calm for several hours; a dead calm off Bray Head; a leading wind to Bray, when it flew slap in my teeth; and then all round the compass, just as I was endeavouring to work through the sound between Dalkey Island and the Muglin Rocks. The wind headed me when through the sound, being nearly due west, and very squally, until within a mile of Kingstown, when a very powerful squall called for instant attention. Down came the mainsail. Would the boat lie-to under the mizen and jib? Naturally not, because the jib, being the balance of the two sails, was far too powerful for the mizen, and bore the bow rapidly to leeward. *Ergo*, down came the jib, and we lay-to under the mizen until it was over. A number of schooner yachts disappeared into the utter blackness of the squall, and emerged with only a scandalised foresail or mainsail, and making straight for the harbour. I reefed down instantly the wind allowed me to loosen the lashing of the mainboom, hoisted a pilot jack, but made the harbour by myself, and brought up. My anchor had not been down three minutes before I heard—"You cannot lay there, sir; this part is all kept clear for accommodation." *The Kate* was therefore handed over to the guidance of the waterman, whose attention I called to my pilot jack, and was told that amateur yachtsmen were always flying pilot flags, and consequently no notice was taken of mine.

The Kate was brought up right in front of one of the large yacht clubs, and a number of glasses were instantly levelled at the boat. I was wet through, and thought it very lucky that Kingstown boasted some very first-class hotels, the "Royal Marine" offering me a refuge in which to change to a dry suit.

There seems to be a wonderful diversity of opinion about heaving boats or vessels to. Ninety-nine amateurs out of a hundred wind up their summary by advising the lashing of the helm, thereby showing that they do not understand the very essence of the question—Why is a boat or vessel hove-to? The answer is, because the master is of opinion that it is not advisable to continue running, on account of the sea. If a boat is hove-to properly *in a gale* of wind, it should always be under stern canvas, with the tiller unshipped, when the body of the boat will hold sufficient wind to cause the seas to be shouldered, instead of being chopped, the boat's head being about four points off the wind. Small craft and large vessels can be hove-to by the head-sails being backed, in any breeze that will allow of such canvas being shown, and the sails should then balance each other. But a boat or other vessel had much better be running on its course in a heavy sea than have its way stopped in such a manner that it perpetually falls off into the trough of the sea, and then flies up to the wind from the action of the rudder. A boat or vessel hove-to in a gale of wind makes *stern way*, with the bow to the sea; but when hove-to for pleasure or convenience, with the foresheets to windward, it forges slowly ahead. A large ship hove-to under a close-reefed maintopsail may or may not require the helm lashed out of the centre; but if some after-canvas was set, there would not be the very great danger of carrying away the rudder, which is incurred by lashing the helm other than amidships. A large ship hove-to in the *open sea* may be assisted by the helm being lashed out of the centre; so that if the bow is thrown to leeward by a heavy sea, the rudder will cause the vessel to come-to again; but the lashing of a helm in a *tideway* depends upon whether the vessel or boat is riding to the tide or to the gale. The pressure of the tide is uniform, and often overcomes the variable pressure of the gale. I will suppose the tide to be running north in a northerly gale: an attempt to lie-to under canvas would throw the vessel into the trough of the sea, and make it head east or west, with a most eccentric motion, as the tide and wind yielded to each other in turn. The practical seaman knows what to do instantly; he will not lash his helm in a tideway other than in the centre, but if he has a drogue he will throw it out on his weather-bow, giving it as much rope as is necessary to compel the bow to the wind. If he has no drogue, or such is not powerful enough, he will lash a spar along the foot of a sail, another along the head, secure each firmly with a strong rope, and throw the sail overboard. The boat or vessel will then lie-to, head to wind, the *stern way* keeping a constant strain on the drogue or sail afloat off the weather-bow. It may be advisable to haul the sail in at the change of tide, but it must be put out again if the gale continue through the next adverse stream.

I stayed at Kingstown until Thursday, and the following interesting conversation took place on Tuesday evening, I think, but I will not be certain of the day. I was discussing the weather with the waterman in charge, when an off-hand sort of an individual asked for my name, following up the request by saying that he was an official of the club, and had to board all yachts and gather information about the owners, so that the club might judge if they were fit people to send invitations to. He then went on to inform me that he had a beautiful little room downstairs; and would I step down and write my name and address? I allowed him to run on so far, and then informed him that if he wanted to know my name and address, he would be able to get all information at the Royal Marine Hotel, to which I quietly departed, leaving him quite thunderstruck with astonishment. I presume people must be mean enough to creep into clubs by the backstairs, or else I would not have received the invitation; it is very certain that every mirror has its reflection, but some are uncommonly green.

A carpenter re-caulked the open seams on Wednesday morning, after which they remained water-tight. I put out in the afternoon, about 6 P.M., for Howth, but fate ordained that I should not leave Kingstown till next day; for I discovered, when off the harbour's mouth, that I had forgotten my oars and boathook, which Callaghan had put into his boat when washing down the decks, and had forgotten to replace. I sent a man back, but he forgot the boathook, and had to journey all the way back again for it. Considerable time was lost, but *The Kate* proceeded to beat to Howth, and had gained some two miles off the harbour when a little driving sleet reminded me that I had left my monkey-jacket at the Royal Marine Hotel. I therefore put back, and sent Callaghan's lad up to the hotel for the coat, which was given to him.

The harbour of Kingstown is the only one I have ever put back to; it is very doubtful whether I could have made Howth or not, with the wind and tide against; but I could have made a small harbour about one mile east of Kingstown, and would most certainly not have returned, except to recover the coat.

I had an opportunity of trying *The Kate*'s sailing qualities against an uncommonly fast Una boat when making Kingstown Harbour for the first time. *The Kate* had a single reef down; so had the Una boat. *The Kate*'s sails were rapidly growing baggy, and on that occasion were very badly set, the mainsail being at least four inches short of its proper hoist. The sail of the Una boat was well set, and seemed to sit remarkably neatly. The Una boat was rigged for bay work, *The Kate* for sea work, so that the proportion of canvas was nothing like equal. The wind was light, the reefs being down simply on account of the late squall, during which the Una boat was in the harbour east of Kingstown, and met *The Kate* about a half-mile from the lighthouse. The boats seemed to sail very fairly together, both being close-hauled. The Una had a little the best of it outside, but walked right away from *The Kate* immediately the shelter of the harbour lessened the small pressure of the breeze.

I left the boat on my return with Callaghan, the waterman, and went to call on a member of the Canoe Club, whose name I unfortunately forgot, and of whose address I was very uncertain; but I made an effort to find the house, as I promised I would call if in Kingstown. I heard on my return that crowds of Irish beauties had been to see *The Kate*. What a loss was mine, for the plucky, warm-hearted Irish character is just the one I most admire in the female sex. I am told the sweet creatures actually struggled to put one tiny little foot on board.

CHAPTER X

FROM KINGSTOWN TO LEITH

FINALLY I left Kingstown on Thursday morning, August 5th, 1869, and made Howth just about tide-time. The wind favoured me as far as Bailey light, where it became most baffling, and at last headed me in earnest as I beat into Howth Roads against a very strong tide, which was running out of the harbour between Ireland's Eye and the main.

The coast line from Bailey light to Howth is excessively bold and craggy, and the tide races round it at a great pace. A large fleet of trawlers were beating up to Howth Roads, to anchor for the tide; and some of them were of great service to me when I was trying to work in, for they showed me where I could go, and saved me the trouble of heaving the lead, which was a great point gained when turning to windward against a strong tide.

I have said little or nothing about the lead in this book, but it had to be hove for all that, more often than I cared about! As a rule, however, I took the boathook, and prodded with that, feeling satisfied so long as I could not touch bottom! This was easier than heaving the lead and quite as serviceable, if not more so, in that with the staff I could have felt the bottom directly, whereas with the lead, a slight loss of time occurs; thus the boathook striking bottom allows the helm to be put down instantly if need be.

I anchored, and got under weigh again at slack water (12 midday), when the whole fleet of trawlers put out. A hardly perceptible air from the SE. blew me to Lambay Island, where I was dead becalmed, and had to row the boat seven miles to the Skerries—a terrible row, because the tide kept setting me into the bay; and I had to get the boat round St. Patrick's Isle by sheer force of rowing—a most difficult performance, as the island is the outermost of three, and extends a long way into the sea. There is an apparent passage between each, but of only a very treacherous depth, and I was very thankful afterwards to think that I had persisted in working round. The position was a dangerous one to the boat, though, of course, not to me; the tide sets very sharply between the islands, and would most certainly have sucked me in had I laboured differently. I had no idea that St. Patrick's Isle ran so far out to sea, and I was taking a line very much within it when off Lambay. A low island running out from the main has a very curious appearance before it fully breaks on the sight. I do not know at what exact distance St. Patrick's Isle can be seen, but perhaps about four miles off, when it will appear just like a dark line, which will gradually grow broader and broader, puzzling the mariner to make out whether it is a racetide or land, till some slight elevation finally determines the point.

The sun was dreadfully hot, and shot down its rays in the most cruel manner. I was very weary when round the point of the island, where, to add to other difficulties, the tide turned against me, and I advanced slowly but surely over it. A gentleman came off in a dingy when I had still a half-mile to row to the harbour, and he kindly sent me a boat, which towed *The Kate* in the last 200 yards. The harbour of the Skerries is a dry one, but very safe when once entered, as it is very much protected by the peculiarity of its position. Its entrance may be said to face the mainland, so that the sea has no chance of rolling into it.

I anchored outside for the night, and departed next morning about half-ebb. The boatman who had towed *The Kate* in the day before came off and gave me a few hints about the coast, which happens to be very rocky to the north of the Skerries. Port Oriel was my destination, and the day's work was a very fair repetition of that on the previous one. Port Oriel has simply a natural entrance between enormous rocks into a very small basin, which nearly dries at low-water. There is just width for a smack to enter. It is not a place for a yacht to attempt, unless compelled; but a pilot is imperative at all times, even for a three-ton boat, and he requires to know the exact position of the vessels inside. If a yachtsman should ever find himself compelled to shelter in Port Oriel, let him rig in his bowsprit before attempting to enter.

The tides off Clogher Point are half-tides, and run very

strong. Clogher Bay looks very inviting, but has not even three feet of water in it. To proceed north from Clogher, it is best to start about half-flood, as the tides divide off Lee Point, the ebb running to the north. I started at 7.30 A.M., and ran before a fine breeze, which increased to a very strong one about 11 A.M., but died away again after 1 P.M. The weather was thick, with strong squalls and driving sleet, and I had to haul up nearly three points, to escape being embayed when passing Dundrum, judging my position by the high land above Annalong, for St. John's light remained a mystery until I was within a couple of miles or so. The coast to Donaghadee is dangerous for a stranger to attempt in thick fog; accordingly, I put into Ardglass, having made a very fair day's work in the strong half gale, before which the boat had been travelling at a great pace. The weather cleared up in the afternoon, but of course I could not foresee that it would do so, nor would I have gained anything, as things turned out, by keeping on. Killough is a much better harbour than Ardglass, but did not suit my purpose so well. I anchored just off the outer harbour, and as I saw several men ashore, I naturally expected some one to offer himself as a pilot. In this I was disappointed, and after waiting more than a reasonable time, and finding that no one came to put me inside, I jumped into the dingy and paddled ashore. I then landed, and saw several men walking up and down the pier or what answered for one, and quite naturally I went up to these seamen, and asked if any of them would lend me a hand to bring the boat to a safe berth inside. My amazement may well be surmised, on my being curtly told by these fishermen (who pranced about like princes) that I and my boat might remain outside for ever, for any assistance I would get from them! Further, their looks implied more than their words! I gave a shrewd guess as to how matters stood, and I promptly replied that I was not a fisherman at all, and that my vessel was not a fishing boat, and that they need not be afraid that I had come over to interfere with their fishing. This mollified them a shade, and they marched up and down their chosen promenade prancing like princes as before, but no further notice did they bestow upon me.

It so happened, however, that another party had been standing by, a mere listener, and he had not spoken a word, but presently he brightened up, after a good look at myself, and to my great satisfaction, he, having a shade more wit, and being also well disposed, said, "I'll put her in a good berth for you," on which the two of us went and brought her in, about fifty yards or so, but an importance distance, in that Ardglass is dangerously exposed in easterly winds.

Naturally I did not care to remain longer than I could help in this hostile locality and decided to be off on Sunday the 7th. The proverb runs: "A Sunday's sail will never fail," and it was fully borne out in my case.

The Bell-buoy

I determined to try and make the Clyde in one big sail from Ardglass! The distance as the crow flies is a probable eighty miles, but as actually sailed it might easily become ninety-five or one hundred miles. I knew that I would have to do a big thing from some other port, even if I miscarried over this, therefore on the principle of not making two bites at a cherry, I put her at it, and on a smiling Sunday morning!

Well, this big thing did not come off—nevertheless the above proverb was verified for all that and in a very remarkable manner, as will be seen!

The wind being WSW., I took a course about two-thirds from the Irish coast and one-third from the Scotch, passing within a yard or two of the bell-buoy off the South Rock. The buoy does not ring as it should do, being evidently very much out of order. The construction of these buoys is peculiar; I had expected to see a bell, and was not a little astonished to find in each case a simple iron cage, with four large iron hammers, which strike alternately as they are swung by the motion of the buoy. I never could see distinctly what it was that produced the sound, although I passed very close to several of these buoys; but I wrote for reliable information, and was answered that it is a bell which differs from an actual bell in having its hammers outside. It is suspended low down in the cage, which no doubt was the reason why I could not make it out.

The breeze, favourable so far, changed just as I passed the buoy, but shifted again to a bare leading wind, which took me within eight miles of the Scotch coast by 12 A.M., and left me becalmed for four or five hours. I will not attempt to define my exact position, for I could not be certain of it; but, at the time, I thought I was somewhere off Port Patrick. I never was in a more provoking calm; vessels passed within a quarter of a mile going four or five knots, before beautiful cats'-paws from the SW. I rowed desperately, first at one and then another, but all to no purpose; wherever I went the calm followed. In the end this was my salvation and the fulfilling of the proverb, though unexpected by myself! The fact was that if I could have caught one of those wild eccentric puffs, there can be no doubt it would have been much worse for me, for I would have kept on all through the night in hopes of fetching the Clyde, and would have been caught in a tremendous and almost endless gale from the north, which lasted with unmitigated fury till Wednesday, reducing large ships to very small canvas, several carrying a foresail only. As it was, after all my comrade ships had departed utterly out of sight, I still lay becalmed and wondered what it all meant, and what I should do.

The Irish coast about Donaghadee was plainly visible till midday, but a detestable haze came over the land and it was entirely hidden, while *The Kate* was drifting till about 4 P.M., when I suddenly sighted the Copeland light, distant about two miles, and bearing NW. by W. My motto towards evening is, "Any port in a calm"; consequently the oar was put out and the boat's head pointed in the direction of Donaghadee, which still remained undistinguishable. A smart breeze from the SE.

enabled me to practise catching the commencement of the stroke, for, as experience taught me that women are not the only fickle things on the earth, I might have often been seen paddling rapidly, even with a fresh breeze and smooth water, when any definite point was to be gained. It was most provoking that Donaghadee could not be seen, for, from wanting a bearing, I had to stand off and on for some little time while the Copeland was again obscured, and thus lost the breeze; for when I obtained a correct bearing, I found myself in another calm, and still some six miles from the harbour, which promised a long weary row. The splendid speech of Eneius occurred to me on these occasions, and often cheered me on when I felt much inclined to let things slide and smoke a pipe.

> O socii! (neque enim ignari sumus ante malorum,)
> O passi graviora! dabit Deus his quoque finem.
> Vos et Scyllaeam rabiem penitusque sonantes
> Accêstis scopulos; vos et Cyclopea saxa
> Experti; revocate animos, moestumque timorem
> Mittite; forsan et haec olim meminisse juvabit.
> Per varios casus, per tot discriminia rerum,
> Tendimus in Latium, sedes ubi fata quietas
> Ostendunt; illic fas regna resurgere Trojae.
> Durate, et vosmet rebus servate secundis.—*Æneidos* i. 198–207

TRANSLATION.

> 'My comrades, who have borne much greater ill—
> The fight, the siege, the blighted ties that kill:
> As Jove has healed the wounds which purify,
> So he will make our trials dignify.
> O ye! who sailed by Scylla's furious race,
> Her roaring rocks, and saw the Cyclop's face,
> Dismiss your mournful fear! Some fireside
> May find you joying o'er the death defied.
> We steer to Latium through a sea of woe,
> Where fates have promised Troy shall tread the foe.
> Endure, and reap rewards!'

I always reaped the reward—first of all, in the comfort of a port; secondly and mainly, in the peculiar satisfaction which can only be felt as the fruit of perfect self-reliance. To make a port was a point of honour, so as to reduce things to a principle, for a happy-go-lucky style reflects no credit. I should have considered it a disgrace had I ever flinched from the toil necessary to place the boat in a position commanding either safety or a chance of beating off to sea. This latter point is of the very greatest importance; so much so that I never dreamed of casting anchor to stop tide without considering the particular winds fatal to the place, and choosing such position that the boat might beat off, let the wind be from any quarter.

The inexperienced reader will doubtless wonder how *The Kate* was off the Copeland; in fact, the questions I have been asked by people utterly ignorant of the action of tide show how excessively hazy the ideas of landsmen in general are on the subject. The usual half query, half assertion was, "You heave-to, of course, when you want to sleep?" The stunning influence of such a question is about as hard for a landsman to understand as it is for him to realise the possible contingencies of sleeping in a tideway. The ordinary idea seems to be that tides are very sluggish, and run as straight as Oxford Street; whereas the very reverse is the case, as may be judged from the fact of the tide having swept *The Kate* from off the Scotch coast to the Copeland, about ten miles. I will just suppose the calm to have lasted, and the crew to have slept. The remaining flood would have carried the boat to the southward of the Copeland, and the return ebb would have put it ashore to a certainty, most likely against some rock in the race, when it would have been rolled over and cracked up like a nutshell. A man should be able to keep awake and do what is necessary for sixty hours, at the end of which time he must either be in soundings and let go an anchor where it will hold, or be some twelve miles from any land before he goes to sleep.

Another fair wind carried *The Kate* into the race off the Copeland, when the breeze suddenly shifted dead ahead. I have noticed the current of air change in the neighbourhood of races, and cannot help thinking that the rush of water is the immediate cause; the why is, I confess, a mystery. The race in question is marked to the north of Mew Island in the chart, but extends to the south of the Copeland, in the fairway to Donaghadee Harbour. The steamers take a course to the north of Mew Island, and through the Copeland Sound, on purpose to avoid the race; but it is a very smooth-water affair, although the tide is very hot. I went about right in the middle of it, and beat into Donaghadee Harbour, where the waterman told me that the Copeland race was not dangerous at any time. The boat was such a perfect dripping-well by the time that I arrived at Donaghadee, that sleeping on board was decidedly dangerous, causing me to awake on the last few mornings and feel rather less like an india-rubber ball than usual, from the intensity of the damp—a state of things which rendered it advisable to sleep ashore for a night or two, and undergo the process of a rum bath.

I will not assert that rum is the best cure for rheumatism—brandy may be just as good; but I have tried the one, and can answer for it. I took the hint from an accident I met with, years ago, when in Cashmere. I was on a fishing tour, and commenced operations on a day when the river was full of snow water. No ladies being present, I enjoyed wading up to my waist throughout the day, wearing the equivalent of a ballet dancer's muslin. The consequence was, that I awoke in the middle of the night to find that the sun's rays had taken a revenge on delicate material, and had swollen my legs and thighs to such an extent that I could not put my foot to the ground for three days, and eventually lost a fortnight's fishing. I had some very strong rum with me, and found my sole relief in using it as an outward application; the rapid evaporation causing a delicious sense of coolness to the skin.

The first symptom of rheumatism which affected my very elastic energies occurred during the first week from London. I instantly had a rum bath on board, at the risk of being discovered by the many charming visitors, and escaped rheumatic pains until my arrival at Donaghadee, where I repeated the operation in the hotel with a like effect, and can strongly recommend the charm. The rum should be rubbed in for at least twenty minutes.

I met with great civility in Donaghadee; in fact, the word kindness would not be out of place. The gale rendered it necessary to lay out the chain cable, and the boat was made as secure as possible, both anchors being down; but some stupid or other fastened another boat in such a position that its stern bumped against and broke the end of my bumpkin, which had not been rigged in, because the boat was moored in such a position as would have precluded the idea of another laying astern, except in the brain of a fool. The first spar that *The Kate* carried away was the starboard oar, which fell overboard just off the Copeland race, as I went forward to lash the mainboom; and it gave me an exciting chase. I very nearly lost sight of it, but eventually was heartily glad to shake hands with what had been a very faithful friend.

An old woman at Donaghadee beguiled me into eating a quantity of unripe gooseberries, which had their usual effect, and that, too, just as the gale finished and I might expect the wind round from the south. I had intended to start on Thursday night, but the weather was so distressingly wet that it was useless to put out. I was obliged to keep awake to watch my chance, and rolled a very large rug around the disturbed organs, so as to preserve them from getting cold. The night was excessively dark, and for the first time I had neglected to put up my riding light, for, being on board and awake, I thought there was no necessity. But I heard a peculiar noise underneath the boat, as I smoked a pipe under the main-hatch, and I quickly discovered it to be the stern line of a smack, which had just come in, and was lying much too close to *The Kate*, threatening every minute to carry away my bowsprit. The men were a very bad-tempered lot, and at first refused to move; but on my giving them to understand that I should hold them responsible for any damage, they thought better of it, and moved off a little. I was just too smart for them; for I heard them say, "Oh, it does not matter, he has no light up"; on which the lamp was instantly lit, and hung up before they had time to make their stern rope fast. That little difficulty had been settled about an hour, when it occurred to me to take a trip outside the harbour, about 1 A.M., in a small boat, and see how the weather was progressing. The appearance of a fine morning instantly caused an itching to lift the anchor and moor *The Kate* to a buoy in the centre of the harbour, where the sails were hoisted and everything put in readiness for an instant start. Two smacks were bound for Cambeltown, and I determined to wait till they were off, as they would be a guide through the sound—a very great consideration on a pitch dark night. There was little or no air to start with till after 2 A.M., when the smacks suddenly departed, the virtue of a number of hands becoming wonderfully apparent. One hauled on the halyards, another on the cable, a third put an oar out, and both vessels were outside in about ninety seconds. *The Kate* followed as quickly as possible, but the low sails were perfectly becalmed in the habour, so that the smacks gained a great advantage, which I lessened considerably by taking a cut through the sound they dared not attempt. I could not sight the buoy, but just made out the beacon, which I hugged so that I might have touched it with an oar, thus getting to windward of the smacks, and gaining so rapidly that I thought I should pick them up; but the strong tide out of Belfast gave their depth of water a great advantage, so that I dropped astern again.

The sailing qualities of my boat were not at their best, not only because I had most stupidly spoilt its trim by adding fifty pounds of lead ballast, so as to put the stern deeper in the water, but also because the canvas had stretched and become baggy (in spite of being hauled out as far as possible), so that the best weatherly course could not be held; nor did the sails feel their former pressure, a large quantity of air escaping through the canvas—all such defects being in addition to the general loss of buoyancy which every vessel undergoes after being for a considerable time in the water, and which will sink her just that one barely perceptible line too many, rendering it necessary to decrease the amount of ballast. In fact, a new boat requires as much attention as a baby, if its best paces are to be discovered.

The two smacks and *The Kate* held a course nearly north close-hauled for several miles, so as to make the most of the remaining tide and be well to windward, should the breeze take an easterly turn. The course from Donaghadee to Lamlash is NE., but the steering such course depends entirely upon the hour of tide in which the vessel starts. I bore away north-east, after making several miles to windward, and could have made Lamlash with the greatest ease, but the breeze set in very strong, and made a bubble in the tideway, which would have drenched me through and through had I persisted in crossing. It must be remembered that I was not quite the thing, and the great object of the day was to keep dry, as a wetting in an inopportune moment might have made me seriously ill.

It is wonderful to hear the different descriptions given of seas. Some men appear to think any little rise on the surface is worthy of the name of a sea, and they talk of them as something fearful in places where it is impossible that large seas can have room to run. The finest sea I ever saw in my life was in 45° S., where the vessel I was in ran under double-reefed topsails before a heavy westerly breeze, which lasted for ten days or a fortnight. The ocean was one mass of huge white breakers, from the largest description of wave that is met outside the Gulf Stream. I should suppose they averaged twenty-four feet in height—that is, twelve above the level and twelve below. I have beaten down Channel from the Downs to the Land's End, under double-reefed topsails the whole way; I have crossed the Channel to Jersey at least a dozen times, and sometimes in as heavy gales as the steamers are in the habit of facing. But I have never seen anything like the same description of sea much to the east of Start Point, nor do I believe that such can possibly run in the Channel fairways. The Channel seas are short, of no great body or height, but very distressing to a vessel beating to windward, as they cause heavy plunges, by throwing a great part of the ship out of the water. I remember, when crossing in the steamer commanded by Captain Goodridge, a sea hung the vessel right amidships, and the fall was so sudden that the chairs actually went from underneath the sitters, who had to pick themselves up the best way they could; but I do not believe that the said sea would have measured fifteen feet. The seas that I met on my passage to Lamlash were very round, short, and perhaps eight feet high—just the seas calculated to upset a boat when running fast across them; because, if pressed too hard, it is sure to overrun the small round tops, and tumble on beam-ends into the hollow. The seas were like a lot of large casks, from the velocity of the tide. Neither before nor since have I ever been impressed in the same manner with the idea that I was about to sail over a succession of barrels. *The Kate* fell on her beam ends twice, when I took the hint, and reefed the mainsail. I also altered my course to ENE., thus shirking the tideway, and skirting the edge of the main tide, and in this manner I made Ailsa Craig, and also contrived to keep dry.

The Craig is a rocky island, of great height; and is famous for its sudden disappearance—in fact, it goes out, as it were, like an extinguished candle. I saw it totally disappear at least a dozen times; and on some occasions when I was distant not more than a couple of miles. I learnt, on enquiry, that no vessel has ever been known to be wrecked on it, though the fearful squalls that strike down off it have dismasted many. They whistled down with extraordinary violence on to *The Kate*, and gave me great cause to rejoice that my gear was so good, for they threatened destruction to the mainsail or mast as I opened the North-East end of the Craig. The breeze carried me off Ayr by 3 P.M., when it left me becalmed for at least two hours, to my intense disgust, as I had hoped to make a very long run before dark. I presume I had travelled nearly seventy miles, if not more, which was very good work for the little boat. It is forty-five miles in a direct line from Donaghadee to Pladda Point (by *Manx's Guide*), and perhaps fifteen more into Ayr; but I did not sail in a direct course, which proceeding made the distance greater.

I did not like the looks of Ayr, and therefore held on for Troon; but the wind was dead ahead, and so very strong that to persist was to receive a ducking, after all; so I put up my helm and ran before a magnificent breeze to Ayr, and was shown in by a fisherman. The harbour is one of the street order, being nothing but the mouth of a river, and is difficult to enter. *The Kate* was fastened alongside a coaster called *Novelty*, a very proper place, as I told the captain, for it placed the two novelties together. I dined ashore, but slept on board, in spite of the damp. I forgot to examine the inside of the boat in London, but I did so at one of the ports a very little to the north, and observed that, in spite of my opening the main-hatch on fine occasions, the inside retained its state of beady perspiration.

I was off early on the morning of the 14th, but the wind

eddied throughout the day in a manner sufficient to drive any sea-going mariner into a lunatic asylum; in fact, pond-sailing is not at all to my taste, and I know no other term to suit the island navigation of Scotland. The tug-steamers were buzzing about all the day, hauling first one and then another vessel out of sight.

Having no wind that I could depend upon I determined to enter Irvine, and bargain for a haul up the river Clyde to Bowling. I entered Irvine by myself, a very unwise proceeding; but I could not fall in with a boatman. The harbour is a narrower street than any I had been in; and, what is worse, has a turn in it. My first danger arose from meeting a steamer towing a large vessel out, just at the corner. I went clear, luckily, but with very little to spare. I then held on until my astonished vision suddenly saw a rope hauled taut right across from side to side. The kedge made a journey instantly, but I might as well have swam alongside and have tried to hold the boat; for, although I had been becalmed outside throughout the day, a strong draught was blowing down the harbour, which propelled *The Kate*'s forestay slap against the rope, the kedge having dragged over the hard sand or through the mud (I forget which). Two little boys most handily ran a stern line out for me, picked up the kedge, and laid it down again where it would hold, so that I got out of the difficulty pretty well; but the suddenness of the whole affair shows what risk attends the want of a hand on entering harbours. The rope belonged to a smack, which chose that awkward moment to haul afloat. I made arrangements for a tow to Bowling Bay, started with the night tide, stopped at Greenock for letters, and lashed alongside a barge in Bowling about 10 A.M. on August the 15th.

I then posted a few lines to friends, informing them of *The Kate*'s passage from Donaghadee. I wrote up my log, and went to bed about nine, but had forgotten a most important epistle; consequently I dressed again, wrote and posted the letter. The post-office was about a mile and a half distant. The landlady offered to send the letter, but I preferred walking, and while doing so I became aware that the great idea amongst the young Bowlings was to bowl along as fast as possible on a stout pair of legs, which excitement seemed to send the rest of the world into a blue funk; for I asked one individual the way to the office, which was only a few yards ahead, but the canny one no doubt thought I was either the devil or one of his imps, and retained an obstinate silence. The night was very dark, and either this person was deaf and dumb—against which proposition the odds are very heavy but for all that it might be so—or else he thought Satan was abroad. However, I did not find his volcanic highness and he neither clawed my letter away, nor enabled one of the active "Bowlings" to overhaul the crew of *The Kate* on the return route. Patter, patter, pat! from the enemy, creating an instant haul at the leg gear. I then returned to bed, having had no more than five hours' sleep during the last eighty-eight, namely, from 7 A.M. on Thursday till 11 P.M. on Sunday, the bare five hours being at Ayr.

The harbour master took a great interest in *The Kate*, and kindly procured me a couple of hands to take the boat through the canal. The journey takes about a day and four hours, two men being of greater service than one and a horse, for the stronger animal would be apt to injure the boat at the locks; and hurry is a useless expenditure of labour, for the simple reason that the locks are chiefly close together, so that the pace of the leading barge will regulate that of the whole fleet, for there is no time to catch up and pass. The men I had with me were considered the two smartest hands on the canal, and I paid for their extra smartness by giving them 17s. each, instead of 15s., the usual fare. I discovered on entering a lock that they were ignorant of the chief essential—namely, which sluice should be opened first, and the way to open it. Had a weak boat of the same size been subjected to a like pressure to that forced *The Kate* against the side of the canal in the second lock, it would have resembled a sieve ever afterwards.

I had no experience in taking a three-ton boat through small confined locks, and was at a loss to know what was wrong at first, though I quickly found out the correct move. To take a large boat through the Bowling, or any other similar canal, see that the stern rope is made properly fast, the head rope likewise, before allowing a sluice to be opened. Then make one

122

hand jump in, to bear the bow off the side, and be careful that the other opens the sluice on the side that the boat is lying, and opens it gradually, for the rush of water in a deep lock, from a fully opened sluice, is calculated to snap the lines, and severely injure, if not capsize the boat; on which any one may rest assured that all the spectators will become aware, just too late, that some one is drowning. It certainly is extraordinary how men can go on doing one and the same thing year after year throughout their lives, and yet never grasp the correct line of action. After the danger in the second lock I got through the canal in safety and without any more especial alarms, in that I took care to direct the proceeding myself at each and every lock throughout the rest of the journey.

Once through the canal, I left Grangemouth about 11 A.M. in tow for Leith. A boat, if properly attached, will steer itself when being towed. To fasten it so that it shall steer itself, take a double turn round the mast, lash two bights in front of the bowsprit, and have them fastened on each quarter of the steamer, being careful that the same pressure is retained on each, and that the bights are well protected with chafing-gear. If comfort is wished, on no account tow behind a fast steamer; if such a course is necessary, and the vessel be a single screw, tow to one rope from the starboard quarter, and steer off that quarter, when a dry passage may be secured; but a ducking will be the consequence of getting on the port quarter. The reason is, that the action of the screw, from left to right, throws the water up on the left.

I was disappointed with the scenery of the Firth, but it would be useless for my rapid survey to attempt a description of the glorious, appealingly-beautiful Clyde. There is a *grand domesticity* about the Clyde and its vicinity! Bachelors who will not marry on even ample means, but prefer the exalted social position conferred by a few broken-down hunters, a heather or two, and a whole mirage, to the despicable contentment only to be found in some faithful heart, should sail up and down the Clyde until their one latent spark of domesticity ignites their one hidden higher attribute, and they awake to the folly of feeding on the dreariness of existence.

CHAPTER XI

FROM LEITH TO BRIDLINGTON

I ARRIVED at Leith in due course, and the boat was safely berthed alongside of the quay, after which I took a turn round the noble city of Edinburgh, which I admire very much, and then returned to Leith, to start on Thursday, the 19th. A wretched calm prevailed till evening, when a light northerly air induced me to make Cockenzie. I met a large lugger, bound for the deep sea, about one mile off the harbour, and mention the fact just to show how easily collisions may occur. I hove-to exactly in the lugger's course, and waited for it to pass, so that I might gain information about the depth of water in the harbour. A lugger will not pay-off very well; the one approaching was close-hauled, and the steersman came too near, in spite of my warning to him to keep further off. The consequence was, that the lugger struck *The Kate* right amidships; and had there been a powerful breeze, the little boat would have been rolled over; as it was, my rail was cut the whole way along, but the mahogany escaped damage. I was told that I would find sufficient water in the harbour, but, preferring my own judgment, I anchored a quarter of a mile off, pulled ashore in the dingy, and found the depth merely a few inches. An invitation to dine necessitated a rapid return to the yawl, to fix the riding light, lock-up the hatches, and make things generally snug.

I met my host at the harbour, a fine grey-headed veteran, who took an honest interest in *The Kate*, from having sons both in the Navy and Army. A pleasant assemblage of ladies made the evening pass away very cheerfully, when, soothing tea having acted as a rigging-cup, I again paddled the dingy off to the shining riding light. I was lying at anchor, about a quarter of a mile out, entirely by myself, and the peculiar watchful feeling I have mentioned above was in active force, so that I had to snatch a snooze between the wakeful starts.

The moon was shining brilliantly at twelve, and a strong breeze was blowing from the west; but I did not start, because the coast between Cockenzie and North Berwick is peculiarly dangerous, from rocks of all description; and I wanted daylight in order to see what I was about. I started about 3 A.M., and joined a lugger off Cullen Point, which had been lying nearly becalmed all night, about two miles from where *The Kate* had been at anchor. The crew were surprised at hearing me mention a strong breeze at Cockenzie, but experience has shown me that such can be perfectly local. The lugger showed me a short cut through the reefs, and we parted company off Berwick. I hugged the shore very close, as the tide was against me, and the rocks are steep-to, which expression means that there are no sunken ones, or awkward ledges running out from those that appear above the surface. The Bass Rock has a grand appearance, and looks as if a succession of steps had been carefully carved on its south-western outline.

The wind freshened into a strong breeze, but fell calm when I was opposite Dunbar, and then chopped suddenly to the south-east, directly in my course. I therefore put into the old harbour, but shifted into the new one, which has been lately made to suit the fishing trade, enabling the boats to get out at any time of tide. The new harbour has a double entrance—that to the north-west being a natural division of rock, very narrow and hard to find; that to the south-east passing under a bridge, which has to be lifted for any vessel with a mast. The harbour is therefore next to useless as a place of refuge for any but those very well acquainted. The men at Dunbar were all engaged in the herring fishery, and were making a very good thing of it.

I dined at the George Hotel, and tendered a cheque in payment, but the landlord looked on it as a kind of joke, and nothing could persuade him to cash it. I had quite enough money to pay with, but determined I would not, for the landlord had no right to refuse, considering that the boat was lying as actual proof of my statement. The old boy quite chuckled when I promised to forward the amount, as much as to say, he thought being "done" rather amusing than otherwise; in fact, he was so good tempered that it was impossible to take offence, and I departed, bowed out with sundry patronising bursts of merriment. I paid the amount in stamps very shortly.

The harbour of Dunbar was left at 1.30 A.M., *The Kate* creating a new sort of sensation among the fishing-smacks by her brilliant port and starboard lights. Sailing at night is the most charming of all charming loneliness—it brings out in full force the intense delight of a perfect self-reliance; but the cream of pleasurable excitement is arrived at only when beating to windward in a fog, with a perfect crowd of steamers dashing about, fog-horns resounding through the air, the coast line indented and utterly unknown. Such was the peculiar characteristic of my nightly navigation along the north-east coast. I carried a nice breeze from Dunbar, and rounded St. Abb's Head at dawn, the dreaded headland of the north, as Flamborough of the east. The tides divide off St. Abb's, the flood running to the south, at a speed that knocks up a strong race bubble, and dashes in among the detached masses of rock, which give the headland such a peculiarly unmerciful appearance, the rocks being perpendicular, and so smooth that the unfortunate ship-wrecked foot would only slip, the fingers fail to grasp. The coast is iron-bound for miles to the north, and is a mass of rocks to the south as far as Eyemouth, where the high land is left astern, the breeze freshening in consequence, to the great gratification of the coaster.

The Kate flew along at a great pace past Berwick, but was nearly becalmed shortly afterwards, just when approaching the many dangers of Holy Island and the Farnes, by far the most dreaded port of the north-east coast. I was repeatedly advised to take a pilot through, or, what is just the same thing, engage another craft to sail in company; but I determined I would find my own way, the last device being one which I should never dream of resorting to. To attempt to pass Holy Island in a calm is perhaps as dangerous an experiment as a single hand can undertake, if from the direction of Berwick, because the island runs a long way out, and the tide is strong, creating a great danger of being set ashore.

A light air had sprung up about east, allowing *The Kate* to progress a little, close-hauled, but heading two or three points to windward of Emanuel Head. The oar, as usual, cut the difference, and took me off the point into a stalk calm, whereon I paddled away for Holy Island Harbour; but the fickle breeze chopped round again to a favourable quarter, and *The Kate* bowed a departure towards North Sunderland. I would have to inflict pages of the *Pilot Book* in an attempt to give an idea of the vast amount of dangers lying between the Farne and Berwick, from rocks, shoals, and strong racetides. It seems to me a miracle that I escaped them all, passing, as I did, right over shoals, whose ugly rocks could be plainly seen at no great depth below the surface. The tide swept me along at a great pace, some of the racetides giving me much uneasiness, because they looked for all the world like reefs of rocks running right across my course; an optical illusion caused by the intense brilliancy of the reflection on the water, and one which occurred in no other place. I had to paddle my way along (for the breeze was merely local), and I was very glad to throw my anchor down off Sunderland pier. It may be useful to yachtsmen to know that the Farne offers about the very best anchorage in heavy north-easterly gales—the land to the south-west being a high steep cliff, and the holding-ground excellent.

A few words from the *Pilot Book*, published by James Imray & Son, will show what is thought of the navigation of these islands. Page 28, "General Caution: It cannot be too earnestly impressed on the minds of all who have charge of vessels passing this intricate navigation (except the constant traders to and from Berwick) not to involve themselves among these islands either by day or night, with favourable or contrary winds."

The harbour master recognised *The Kate* at once, came off, and put me ashore, the boat taking care of itself outside until my return in the evening. The landlord of the Shepherd Inn cashed my cheque instantly, thus showing the great difference between men.

The herring fishery was paying very well at Sunderland, though the year was not favourable for sea fishing generally. I left Sunderland at tide-time on Sunday morning. There was not a sign of life in the harbour when I lifted my anchor, but as

I was approaching a dangerous rock called the Grimstone, I saw a Sunderland boat creep round the point (which I had left astern), watching, no doubt, to see me strike; but I passed quite clear, at a distance of at least twenty yards from the sunken danger, and eventually made Boulmer Basin about 4 P.M., around which I cruised in the most reckless manner, hunting for a patch of sand to drop the anchor on, the whole place being apparently a mass of rocks. Great liberties may be taken at high-water, which would have a most disastrous consequence at a wrong moment, especially in a place like Boulmer, which is of all places one of the most difficult to enter and depart from. It is a natural harbour, formed by rocks, which all but join, leaving a passage of about ten or twelve yards as a rapid swashway for the tide. I was ignorant of the passage, but was lucky as to the time of tide in which I ventured over the rocks on my first entrance; but the sight of them at low-water showed me plainly the great risk I had run, and I was careful to go out the correct way. The wind was ahead on Monday morning; not that its direction was paid much attention to as a rule, but I had an awkward passage to make to the Tyne, which rendered it advisable to start under favourable conditions.

The crew felt some slight curiosity to see Alnwick, and departed in tow of a land steamer, breakfasted, and returned to sail about 5 P.M., in hopes of making a long leg to Hartlepool. The wind was light, the glass rather low, and the weather anything but encouraging; consequently *The Kate* was made snug for the night by a reef throughout, the mizen being stowed in addition, so that my riding light could be shown if a steamer was coming on rapidly astern. I reefed down, not immediately on account of the weather, but because of the immense number of smacks, coasters, and steamers, which might make it awkward work having to reef in the dark, and the night was excessively so.

I was well to the east of Coquet Island at 7 P.M., and then took a course so as to pass some two or three miles from Tynemouth. The wind dropped to a very light breeze, but the fog was so dense that I could not sight the Tyne revolving light until abreast of it, at 3 A.M., when it occurred to me I had much better make the harbour than remain out on such a coast when it was impossible to see. I stood in within a short distance of the harbour, but could not make it out, on account of the volumes of dense black fog, which hid everything from view, the furious rush of steamers on every side betraying their presence by the sound of the paddles or screw.

I have said little about the cooking on board, and it may be imagined it was just the thing that I did not relish. I had terrible fights at first to keep plates, knives, and forks clean and serviceable, but after leaving Southampton I put them all in the locker, where they remained for the rest of the voyage, and contented myself with two large cups, which answered every purpose. The tins of meat contained nearly half a pint of soup or gravy, which, if poured into a soup plate, made a greasy diversion on each side, according to the motion of the boat. The cups were easily cleaned, besides presenting other advantages, the hot water in which the tin was cooked being used for that purpose. Every description of ordinary knife and fork was laid aside, large salad forks and spoons being found by far the most useful; but the fork requires to have one prong neatly cut off, otherwise a whole salad fork would be found inconveniently large for the mouth.

The lamp used was that usually known as the Russian spirit lamp; and having tested its utility as fully as possible, I have no hesitation in saying that it is an excessively dangerous article to have on board for constant use. Its manner of burning is most eccentric: sometimes it will throw up a perfect hurricane of fire, which can be heard roaring at a considerable distance; at others, though trimmed in precisely the same way, it will burn in an enormous sluggish column of flame, which rolls out into the well with the lurch of the boat, threatening to set fire to everything. Now and then it varies the entertainment by becoming a fountain, shooting the spirit up from inside, which falls into the tin case, creating a perfect mass of fire outside the lamp, necessitating an instant attention with a teacup full of salt water. Again, the fire is such that it persists in coming out at the handle, in spite of extra washers and the tightest screwing, creating a great difficulty in putting the lamp out. But the

worst feature arises from the fact of the spirit being shaken out
of the cuts in the bottom (which are intended to allow a free
current of air), compelling constant attention to the furnace if
there is any bubble on, because the whole chamber will be a
mass of flame in an instant, and must be put out. I have taken
the trouble to mention these peculiarities, for they cease to be
dangers when known and properly met. I cannot recommend

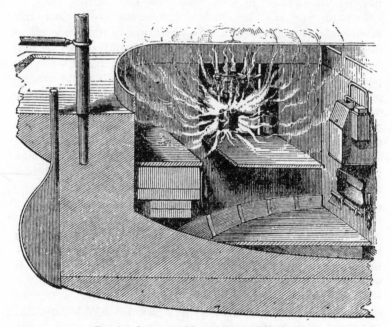

Russian lamp, cooking-place, and well, etc.

the lamp, and know of nothing to take its place; but let the
engineer be careful that he burns spirit *which water will extinguish*. The lamp was in one of its most bumptious, upsetting
humours; and the attempt to cook tea and boil some eggs about
3 A.M., off the Tyne, ended in *The Kate* being nearly set on fire.

Some pilots hailed, to know if I wanted to be shown in; but
I said, "No," determined to give the fog a chance of lifting.
Later on, as the tide was about to turn against me, I hailed a

pilot, who put me in for the sum of three and ninepence. The man had hardly taken charge before a powerful breeze blew the fog away, and gave us a hard beat into the harbour. The tide runs out very strong, and was at that time on the ebb, so that I shook the reef out of the mainsail, to give the boat a fair chance of turning to windward over the tide, which it did in first-rate style, to the great satisfaction of the pilot, who said he had fully expected to be obliged to fasten on to a steamer.

I would on no account advise a single-handed stranger to attempt the anchorage off the pier without a pilot, even under favourable conditions, but certainly not on the ebb and with a head-wind; for if the boat should be carried across the dredgers, the tide would make very short work of it, if there were not sufficient hands to bear off. The strong north-west breeze continued throughout the day; but I am satisfied that it was perfectly local, for the pilot told me it had been blowing just as fresh all through the night, whereas I had been nearly becalmed a few miles off, and I learned next day that the breeze did not extend to Hartlepool. I stayed at the Bath Hotel, which is decidedly the best in the place, and the landlady, Mrs. Jones, is a perfect pattern of a landlady.

The north-wester was still blowing strongly when I put out at twelve (midnight), but it proved itself to be nothing but a strong harbour draught by sailing me into a southerly wind at the distance of one mile from the harbour. That night at sea was (with the exception of the one in the mouth of the Thames) the most enjoyable of all. The weather was thick, so that the lights off Sunderland could only be seen occasionally; vessels appeared and disappeared as if by magic; steamers buzzed about in every conceivable direction, and the coast line remained a solemn mystery until about 5 A.M., when I found that (in spite of numberless tacks, of quietly heading to every point of the compass, as *The Kate* amused herself by waltzing in a calm, while the crew smoked, chatted, sang, and entertained the quarter-deck passengers after the most approved fashion) the land was made exactly in the right place, half way to Hartlepool, and that *The Kate* was in excellent position with respect to other coasters, who had all started at tide-time.

131

I had to make rapid use of the riding light, to warn steamers off (for the side lights cannot be seen astern). It was hung on its usual peg beneath the main-hatch, so that it could be exposed in an instant; however, one steamer came at me end-on whilst I was lying becalmed, without the power to avoid collision, and the consequences would have been fatal but that I seized the riding lamp, ran to the bow, and hallooed every sort of blue murder I could get my tongue round on the emergency. Hard-a-port flew the helm, but the steamer rounded to within five yards of my bowsprit, which might have been awkward had an ugly puff come exactly from the wrong quarter. I had no fog-horn at that time, but procured one at Hartlepool, on the recommendation of the master of the smack I was lashed alongside of.

The land is high to the north of Hartlepool; and although I kept out a mile and a half from it, the conflict of eddy winds was such as I could not have believed possible, actually culminating in the distressing fact of my masthead flag blowing strongly in the right direction, while the jib was aback from an annoying under-current. The oar leaped out in a crack and settled the point, the wind ultimately springing fresh and hard from the south-east, compelling an anchorage until the midnight tide.

Having made Hartlepool I went to the "King's Head"— dined, slept for two hours, returned on board about 10 P.M., and discussed the hurricane of the 15th of June over a pipe with the master of the smack. The vessel, of about 100 tons, was handled by this man and one other only, who were in the constant habit of sailing without further assistance. The gale caught him just off Whitby, where he had such a fine weatherly position as to be able to keep away dead before it for Flamborough Head, but for which stroke of seamanship he would have been wrecked to a certainty, for the mainboom parted and the sails split, which would have rendered a haul to windward out of the question. The professional resources of such men are very great, and they are just the characters to make the best of everything—not only bold, but perfectly fearless: they look upon a heavy gale as a little diversion they are sure to pull through somehow or other. No other seamen would stand a chance alongside of them. It must be remembered that the hurricane in question was about the worst which has ever visited the north-east coast of England. The men all along the coast north of Flamborough told me it was hardly possible to stand on the beach on solid ground, but the gale was not nearly so violent to the south of the head. My visitor informed me that, on the parting of the boom the mainsheet was unshackled and fastened to an iron chain, which they lashed across the stern as a temporary horse; the sail was then close-reefed, the splits being luckily confined to the lower part. He described the sea as one of the worst he ever saw in his life; but he continued to run, rounded the head, and chucked the anchor down right on top of the sands. He and his mate then set to work to mend the mainsail, in spite of the spoondrift, which was flying mast-high; a stitch here, another there, made such improvement that the lion-hearted two raised the anchor on the first lull, and made a splendid run up Boston Deeps. The master was a married man, with a large family—may all his sons be like him! I have, unfortunately, forgotten the name of the coaster, or I would have been proud to mention it.

The Kate took leave of Hartlepool at 12.30 midnight, the master of the smack acting as my pilot outside the very hazardous entrance. The wind was very light, so that I failed to make Whitby in the tide, although I kept three or four miles from the land, on purpose to benefit by the full swing of the current. A hard row enabled me to anchor in a convenient bay (about one mile from the harbour), and gain what is ludicrously called my "second wind." I remember a grand discussion taking place, some two years ago, in the newspapers on the subject of "Second Wind"; but I fancy the world is about as learned on the point as it was before the very active correspondence which was carried on at the time. I shall be quite humble if my view of the case is set aside by medical men, who are the people competent to determine the question. The action of the lung in a healthy subject secretes about one pint of water every twenty-four hours under ordinary exercise; but when extraordinary exercise is indulged, the lung secretes a larger quantity of water than usual in a very short space of time, which water is absorbed throughout the system, and would put an end to all powers of continued action if it did not find an immediate escape. The duty of the skin is to afford the safety-valve required. It throws off the over-secretion of water in the form of perspiration, and frees the lungs, heart, liver, and vascular system, thus allowing the individual to continue his high-pressure exercise. I think it will be found that large-lunged men perspire more than others. Such lungs, joined to a free open skin, are the requisites for severe continued exercise, and will do more towards winning a race in either man or horse than all the muscle put together. I am perfectly certain that all exercises which call for a greatly increased action of the lungs are excessively injurious to life, if persisted in beyond a certain point. There can be no doubt that running is the most killing exercise of all. My own opinion is, that the cause lies in the too rapid expenditure of the air which is in the lung, and is its defence from the common air we breathe; and whenever the change is effected too rapidly, and too often (as is the case in running, to the greatest extent), the lung becomes exhausted and the whole frame weakened.

I got the anchor at four hours' tide, and departing from my snug corner I made Whitby with a head wind, and was towed into the harbour about 6 P.M. Dinner and a two hours' nap refreshed me for another start at 1 A.M. on Friday, the 27th. The dawn ushered in a dead calm, which was most provoking, because I was particularly anxious to make Scarborough in the tide, so as to present a cheque at my cousin's bank before it closed, in order that I might be able to take advantage of the afternoon tide, and then the midnight one. My anxiety was a double one: not only to secure the tides, but to get my money without the risk of having a cheque refused, or, in other words, of being insulted, in addition to a positive risk of being delayed either there or further on.

I passed a large number of herring-smacks a mile or so south of Robin Hood's Bay, and had paddled about one mile ahead of them when I heard a number of fog-horns sounding all over the place. I thought at first the fishermen had hit off a little calm excitement and were blowing for a breeze; but presently I heard the well-known thud of a steamer's paddles, and, to my astonishment, I saw the tug steaming round and round the fishing-boats for some half-hour before laying hold of the tow-ropes. The fog-horns were blown expressly for the steamer, being always recognised on that coast in clear weather as the signal for a tow; but doubtless the fishermen held out as long as they could on the chance of a breeze saving their 15s. The appearance of the steamer was evidence of the great distance at which the fog-horns can be heard, for the steamer was heard long before it was seen, and must have been distant some four or five miles. *The Kate* was being paddled on all the while; but seeing it was useless to hope for Scarborough in the tide, I also blew a challenge on my fog-horn, and joined the band as soon as the steamer caught me up; and a novel sight it was to tow in brigade, as it were, with about one dozen others, each boat keeping its own particular line and never bumping up against another. A want of experience made me blunder, but I suppose it was excusable that in a dead calm I never thought of the sails. They should have been lowered and made fast before I commenced to tow; for had a breeze struck the canvas, it might have caused me to bump against, if not seriously damage the other craft or my own. The crew of *The Kate* intends to know more about it in future; as it was, I had to top the mizen, so as to clear the bowsprit of a following smack, and truly the steering was to half an inch, in one sense. I had to lose only half an inch of ground by allowing my tow-rope to be at too small an angle, and my rigging would have been touched by the pursuing bowsprit—only touched, but fancy the disgrace! I being the last comer, the faintest collision would have been my fault.

I landed at Scarborough, presented my cheque, breakfasted, wrote up my log, and started again at tide-time, to beat to Filey against a stiffish breeze from the south-east. The crew of *The Kate* was received with three cheers by the assembled fishermen of Filey, and was kindly put ashore by a clergyman who happened to be fishing in the bay. The postmaster delivered important despatches, affording a glimpse of the campaign of the world at large, and some of its minor engagements; the plan of the great battle appearing in its usual hazy, undefined state, with slide, written in large letters, underneath: "American Kings and English Presidents in a state of frantic collision, from the blundering mechanism of their skates."

The tide made away round Flamborough Head at 2 A.M., and *The Kate* turned her attention to the negotiation of that hazardous point, after the crew had indulged its usual nap of two hours. It is not at all an easy thing to sail round from Filey to Bridlington, although the water, boat, sails, and crew being ready would seem to present the whole state of the case to a landsman, who naturally might wonder where the stoppage can arise. The distance to the head is ten miles; the set of the tides very awkward, both as regards direction and the number of hours of flood; the winds are very changeable, and when off the land dangerously squally.

I started off with the wind abeam, and threatening to blow the mast out of the boat every five minutes, compelling me to top the mizen twice in the first three-quarters of an hour, lower the mainsail on deck, and run with the jib alone; all of which manœuvres had to be carried out in the darkness, which hid the cliffs from sight, creating a little anxiety from the fact that I knew the tide was sweeping on to the rocks at the rate of four miles an hour. The wind very soon headed me, so that I had to close-haul, and on my very first turn to windward the sister hooks of the peak-halyards flew out, leaving me at a critical moment more at the mercy of the tide than ever. The fore-sheet was rapidly brought to windward, the peak let go, the main lowered sufficiently, everything properly secured, and the sail hoisted again as speedily as possible. The dawn broke, and showed me I was much nearer the cliffs than was pleasant; but the dangerous part of the tide was passed, namely, the set from Filey Brig. This forms a race, running about five miles an hour in the direction of the land. I beat off the head, and met a couple of coasters, who gave me the go-by, as the tumbling sea knocked the light air out of my sails; but they and everything else disappeared in a densely yellow fog, which overtook us before we had time to catch the proper bearing to lead round the headland, *The Kate* and coasters being still to the NW. of the point. They stood away to the east; I tacked slap in for the head, trusting to my judgment of pace and time to enable me to make boards of about the same length, until I should deem myself clear. Had I kept away to the east, I would have been swept round the head again by the tide, in my attempt to work into Bridlington, for the tides by the headland are only half-tides; that is to say, they run for three hours, instead of six, before they turn. The Bridlington men assured me I might consider myself very lucky to have got round on a first attempt.

The thud of paddles kept all the fog-horns going. Mine was of great service to the other coasters, because it showed them they need not fear going ashore, as they were to the east and north of *The Kate*; but I feel convinced that the steamer would have been a wreck but for my warning horn and a providential lift of the fog; for it was steering straight for *The Kate* and dead upon the headland, which was distant about a quarter of a mile. I marked off a number of courses while the fog lasted, and trusted entirely to the compass and my own sense of hearing to carry me round. The awkward part of the affair lay in the difficulty of determining the latitudinal depth of the point; but I guessed it at about a quarter of a mile. Such distance may or may not be right, as I never saw the headland, and obtained only a momentary glimpse of its southern foot, sufficient to show the danger.

I will say a word or two here about charts and their protection. My charts were constantly exposed to damp and positive wet; but I did not lose one. I frequently had to use them when it was raining; I took not the slightest particular care of them, but I treated *them to a principle*. I kept *them whole*, and rolled up in the well, always at hand, using each chart as I wanted it, and then putting it on one side. The consequence is, that all my charts are fit for another voyage. Those of the north-east coast have made several fresh voyages, for I gave them away. I had a chart-frame made in London, with the idea of cutting the charts into pieces and placing each piece in the frame as wanted; but I never once used the frame for its specific purpose, though I found it invaluable as a protection for my compass-card of deviations.

The ebb had begun to make away out of Bridlington for at least two hours before I made the harbour, which time was spent in a weary row over the tide, with the mild assistance of an occasional cat's-paw. The bottom of the boat had collected an amount of weed, which was a great drawback to speed, and made the rowing proportionately heavy, counterbalancing the slack tide of the bay. The harbour (as nearly all on the east coast) is a dry one, which greatly added to my anxiety to make it in time to choose a proper berth, so that the weed might be all removed at low-water. I blew the fog-horn as a signal for a boat from the harbour, for I was rapidly getting exhausted; but none came, as the boys were in the habit of blowing fog-horns all over the place. I therefore ended one of my most distressing rows by throwing the kedge down in the middle of the harbour, and surrendered *The Kate* to the care of a boatman who came on board shortly afterwards.

It may now be understood that in these desperate rows I was in reality racing against time. It was of the utmost importance to me to make this harbour before it dried out. All round the coast, all my comfort depended on this making the harbour and thus it was I had to torture myself at the oar. In this case it was exceedingly lucky for me that I did so, irrespective of ordinary rest and sleep.

CHAPTER XII

FROM BRIDLINGTON TO SOUTHWOLD

THE Britannia Hotel sheltered me for the night, during which a very heavy gale sprang up from the north-east, collecting a fleet in Flamborough Roads, of which I counted seventy-one ships at 5 P.M., but doubtless there were many others I could not see. A large number of fishing-smacks left the roads to shelter in the harbour; but when they had all come in, about 10 P.M., I took *The Kate* outside, anchored off, and slept on board, so as not to be humbugged in the morning by waiting for the tide to float me out of the harbour. I got my usual amount of winks, but not much more, as the strong bubble kept us knocking about all night, and I had to keep a sharp look-out that the riding light worked properly, or I might have been run down. I will not go so far as to say that I could awake to any particular five minutes I wanted to, but at that point of the voyage I could go to sleep with the certain feeling that I would awake if necessary. I do not believe it was possible for a vessel of any sort to approach without my detecting its presence; as for a clincher-built lugger, I could have distinguished it by ear alone from any other sort of craft; its rise and fall in the water being a most snappish, grating sound, which every now and then resembles a prolonged hiss, if the boat is running on a wave.

Monday morning turned out fine, as I had expected, and *The Kate* was soon paying her farewell salutes to the fishing craft, one of which had given me a hail on passing. There was a good tumble on the wave, which grew heavier as I approached the Humber. I made a splendid course slap on to the northern outer buoy which marks the channel up the Humber. I do not think that I was in the correct channel for craft drawing a considerable amount of water; for I noticed the fishing fleet kept away towards the lightship (which lay about one mile on my port bow), while I went through a heavy breaking sea over the

Binks. If one, I presume at least one hundred fishing-smacks wondered at and admired the little boat, as she rose and fell amid the broken mass of white water, causing her crew to smoke a pipe of the greatest satisfaction.

The strong ebb delayed my arrival at Grimsby till about 5 P.M., when I threw down my anchor with a feeling of great pleasure at having made my own way through the many dangerous sands and crowds of vessels which impede the navigation of the Humber. A gentleman (whose name most unfortunately escaped both our attentions at the moment) very kindly found me out at the hotel, and presented me with a special chart of Boston Deeps, which proved of the very greatest service in the navigation of that intricate water. I winked on board till midnight, when I smoked a pipe, waited for the tide to turn, and got the anchor up at 2 A.M., in hopes of making Wainfleet Roads. I had carefully written down the different courses I steered up the river, and their converse took me safely down again.

Perhaps a word of warning may not be out of place. I would advise the single hand to be very careful always to note his courses, either up a river or out of any intricate harbour (such as Harwich) which he may have to re-travel by night. "Oh, but the place is beautifully lit!" Very true; but there are no puzzles to equal the crowd of lights a stranger is unacquainted with. Those of vessels in motion or at anchor add to other difficulties, and, consequently, I recommend the courses as the guide, considered with regard to the different sets of tide, the lights being used as a help.

The Kate almost embraced the African who guards one of the overfalls, but added a good-bye, and chased the whiter swells; admired herself in the mirror of the deep, then bore her locks against the adverse breeze, arriving off Chapel about 5 P.M. The description of Skegness in the *Pilot Book* answered exactly for Chapel, and is far more like the latter than the former—in fact, I read the letters "Chapel" on the chart as meaning some sort of church, but never dreamed of a town or village of the name. I had not met a single craft throughout the day that I could speak, though I had outsailed three large coasters, which were bound for the Deeps, and were taking a course outside the sands, while I was endeavouring to find the anchorage inside them (Virgil's "hospitium arenae") without paying the penalty of running aground. As I could get no information on the water, I determined to try my luck ashore, anchored off Chapel, chucked the dingy overboard, and paddled away. A number of breakers were dashing on the beach, and though of no great size, they rolled in with very great force, twisted the dingy round, and would certainly have upset it, but that I jumped out with the rope in hand, preferring a ducking in order to one on no principle whatever, as I happened to have a chart inside, which might have been lost, had the dingy turned over.

> At pius Aeneas per noctem plurima volvens
> Ut primum lux alma data est, exire, locosque
> Explorare novos, quas vento accesserit oras;
> Qui teneant (nam inculta videt), hominesne feraene,
> Quaerere constituit, sociisque exacta referre.
> Classem in convexo nemorum, sub rupe cavatâ,
> Arboribus classem circum atque horrentibus umbris
> Occulit.—*Æneidos* i. 305-311.

TRANSLATION

> The wakeful prince determined to explore
> The coast at dawn; enquire whose the shore
> And what the race; if man or beast defends
> The seeming waste; and then inform his friends.
> But first hides the fleet within a cove,
> Where rocks embalm the tears of weeping grove:
> And then departs. Achates bears his spears—
> .   .   .   .   .
> The little dingy bore me and my fears.

I hauled the little one high and dry, and walked along the beach until I met a coastguardsman, who made me learned as to Wainfleet Roads, steadied the dingy through the first breaker, watched me safely through the rest, and went his weary way. It was very hard work pulling the dingy clear of the breakers, for the boat is so short and light that the water turns it round in a second, there being no difficulty in describing any amount of circles with it, but great difficulty in rowing it straight in any water. Each breaker went clean over the boat, half filling it, which was a matter of no importance; but had it deviated out of the straight line, the next would have upset the tiny craft before I could possibly have recovered the direction. I met the captain of a coaster hunting for his anchor off Skegness, the gale on Sunday having carried away his cable and nearly hurled his vessel on a sand before he could get the forestaysail set, so as to swing it round into Wainfleet Roads, where I saw it lying high and dry at low-water, marking, with others, what is considered the best spot in the roads, being out of the

The dingy pulling through the surf

tide, and the vessel being safe on the mud six hours out of every twelve.

There are a great many so-called dangers between Wainfleet and the Humber. The *Pilot Book* says, page 39: "Between the Wash and the river Humber are several overfalls and sandy flats, which must be carefully avoided. These are the Clay Huts, Inner Dowsing, Trusthorpe Overfalls, Sheddle Overfalls, Protector Overfalls, Saltfleet Overfalls, Rose Sand, and Sand Haile Flats. Clay Huts are elevations of clay, with a depth of from three to eight feet over them; the Inner Dowsing is a dangerous sand." The overfalls are all described as dangerous; but I know *The Kate* went through a good many of them, and I did not see anything particular. One set (I cannot say which) can be heard roaring miles off, but they did not seem much, in spite of the row they made.

I anchored in Wainfleet at dead low-water, and thus had a good view of the sands, which uncover to a great extent. My usual supply of bread was unfortunately forgotten when I left the Humber, so that I found myself on very short commons, and hoisted my pilot jack overnight, in hopes of attracting the attention of some fishermen who could bring me a fresh stock, and tell me whether I could cross the sands or not at high-water, a little piece of information on which the *Pilot Book* was silent. The captain of the above-mentioned coaster paid me a visit next day, and told me I would find sufficient depth overall at high-water, but cautioned me against attempting Cromer or approaching the land in the heavy surf-sea that was running all along the coast, owing to the late gale and a strong NE. breeze blowing at the time. He departed, and I determined to start with the tide at 12 midnight.

It blew a very strong breeze from the north-east throughout Wednesday morning, Sept. 1, so much so that my friend informed me I had better shift my anchorage, as the sea that was rolling in might possibly snap the cable, or, if that held, wash clean overboard. I trusted the little boat to hold her own somehow or other, assisted her with thirty fathoms of cable in four-fathom water, made every thing as secure as possible, blew up my air-bed, and went fast asleep, leaving the squalls to whistle without an audience. The wind shifted to the westward of north, as I had felt certain and hoped it would do, for one of my courses was ENE. from the Wells lightship to the Docking Channel; but signs of ugly weather presented itself in the shape of a coaster, who had sought the roads in the afternoon, evidently as a refuge. The night was excessively dark, and one of my chief dangers lay in the risk of striking against the buoys which mark the different sands in Boston Deeps. I had to pass within a few yards of one, which lay about 200 yards off my anchorage; and the darkness may be guessed from the fact that, although I most certainly did pass within a biscuit-chuck of the identical buoy, I never caught sight of it, although to touch it with my bowsprit was to become a very proper wreck. I had to pass a number of dangerous sands, one of which was the Dog's-head, and the chance of finding the correct passage may be realised from the information in the *Pilot Book*, at page 36: "The south end of the Dog's-head is separated from the Long Sand by a narrow channel, with from four and a half to six fathoms in it, running first SW. by W., and afterwards W. in Boston Deeps. *It is too intricate for a stranger to attempt.*" The remark applies to daylight; it was therefore useless for me to hope that I would escape the breakers, which render the crossing of the sands more or less dangerous in daylight, as even then the seas might easily wash the helmsman overboard.

I took my course for the Wells lightship quite irrespective of all such matters; and when somewhere about the Dog's-head Sand, I became aware that I was in the surf—a ghost-like whiteness on the port bow, a violent stagger of the boat, the peak gone, the compass knocked off the gimbals, and a perfect deluge of spray introduced me to breaker No. 1, as a gentle hint of what might be expected from No. 2. There was nothing for it but to smoke a pipe, and sail on till dawn. I guessed pretty well what was the matter with the peak; as for the compass, I never expected to right it, for my hand is too large for the doorway. The moon was in the last quarter, and would have shed but little light upon affairs, had there been no murky atmosphere to dim its silvery beams; as it was, it and some of the larger stars answered for a mark for a short time until the clouds obscured the heavens from my sight, and the wind again shifted very ominously to the east of north. I did not continue my course up to the lightship, but hauled to the wind when within a few miles of it, for, as it blew, every foot nearer the lightship was a foot to leeward. The exact course from the light to the Docking Channel is ENE. ¼ E. To find it without the compass, I had only to mark the angle it made with the course I was steering to the light, which happened to be very nearly a right angle, and would necessitate the light being brought dead astern as soon as it came on the beam by the action of the tide. I did not wait for such exactness, but brought it astern gradually, and kept it there until I sailed it out of sight, steering about ENE. ½ E. for a considerable part of the time.

It is not nearly so difficult to steer a course without a compass as many might imagine. A first-rate steersman would make a very fair course by watching the angle of a flag, supposing the wind to be steady, and its quarter known in the first instance; but things are reduced to great simplicity as long as any bearing-point can be seen, such as a light, piece of land, or a constellation, though the latter is not so good as the former. The length of the boat represents sixteen points, so that, when steering straight on to a mark, if it is necessary to diverge four points either one way or the other, the object must be brought before the beam; for eight points it must be brought square to the beam, and this course will soon bring the mark astern as the boat sails on, and supposing the mark tolerably close at starting. These remarks apply to still water; for in a tideway an allowance must be made, which nothing but a knowledge of tides can render practicable.

It was wonderful what excellent headway the boat made in spite of the mainsail being all disorganised, so that in about one hour I had sailed the Wells light entirely out of sight, it being dead astern the last time I saw it. After that, Hunstanton light was the only guide that remained during the later hours of darkness. I cannot say exactly where the boat was at daybreak; I certainly fancied I saw the Docking Channel buoys about dawn, but not near enough for a positive statement. I guessed the land to be about seven or eight miles off at daylight, when, being able to see how matters stood aloft, I hove-to, climbed the mast, and hooked on the peak halyard-block, which had been jumped out of its place. It was not at all an easy matter to hold on sufficiently to put things right, for there was a very nasty sea on; and, so as to give myself a chance, if my own dearly-beloved *Kate* did jerk me overboard, I threw a rope overboard, and let it trail a long way astern, so that if "go" was to be the order of the day, I could still cling to the tail of her garments until she thought fit to round-to, and make friends again. I did the work of dressmaker about as well as might be expected from the state of high spirits the charming creature indulged, and succeeded in replacing the block, though in doing so I gave it a twist the wrong way! However, I did not find that out until I had descended and began to haul

The crew of *The Kate* aloft, hooking on peak halyard-block—mainsail lowered, jib aback, heavy sea

on the peak halyards, on which I was satisfied to leave matters until I should arrive at Yarmouth.

The compass was replaced on the gimbals, with the assistance of the salad spoon, and a SE. $\frac{1}{2}$ E. course led me outside the Blakeney Overfalls, within fifty yards of the bell-buoy, which, by-the-bye, appeared a little down in the mouth, as I heard no sound. The wind increased, blowing very hard in the squalls, causing the jaws of my mainsail to groan in a very threatening manner. The sea was decidedly the heaviest I had ever ran before, and in the neighbourhood of Cromer had a very ugly appearance, taking the form of immense curling breakers, from eighteen to twenty feet high. The excitement of running over these was glorious; the boat ran right on the very edge of some, conveying the idea that, if a plumb-line could be dropped from the bowsprit, it would touch nothing for twenty feet, the decks being a mass of white water as the wave broke, and *The Kate* subsided gracefully into the hollow.

The only comparison that I can make to running before a heavy sea is that of riding across country on a horse that jumps high and wide; the feeling is the same in each case, but only momentary in the jump, whereas the boat may run just on the verge of the wave for several minutes together. The impression is that of never coming down, or a sort of flying in the air, which I well remember, on one occasion, when riding my Arab horse "Monarch" on a sky-larking jumping expedition with a number of officers of her Majesty's 51st and other corps. The horse was jumping very wide, and at last culminated his efforts in a splendid leap, which measured over thirty feet, the obstacle being a double bank, about three feet six inches in height, with a brook running down the centre.*

I was advised to hug the shore on approaching Yarmouth, and not attempt the mysteries of the Cockle Gat. I had passed about one mile from the beach at Cromer, and maintained a like distance past Haisborough to Yarmouth, approaching which I determined to find my way through the Cockle Gat, for several reasons, one of which was, that I was rather proud of navigating the boat by the correct channels; another, that a glance told me there was no passage through Hemsby Hole, for the sea was breaking very heavily all over it. I hit the line of buoys without the least difficulty, steered close up to the Cockle lightship, bore away on the correct course for the roads, and anchored off Yarmouth jetty about 3.30 P.M.

I had not received any letters since leaving Filey, and was naturally anxious to hear; but on going ashore, I found all my letters had gone to Cromer, so that I lost a splendid breeze and

---

* The above jump was not measured from uprights, but an allowance was made by raising the hand: as measured, it covered 32 feet 4 inches, being 35 feet odd to the fore-hoof marks.

a fine flood, which would have put me into Harwich that evening. Still, I had made a capital run of nearly sixty miles, having existed on two biscuits, one of which was served out to the crew at 4 A.M., the other at 2 P.M., when I lay-to for a minute or so to draw a glass of sherry, which was all spilt over the hatchway, and the crew smoked a pipe instead. The spilling of the sherry (the first accident of the sort on board) may be considered the forerunner of all the other bad luck. I started off next day with the tide against me, and too light an air to allow the boat to make much progress.

I had left Wainfleet Roads with a double reef in the jib, as a gale might come on at any moment. The waterman who looked after the boat had (unless I make a mistake between him and Mathew Butcher, my Lowestoft attendant) unhooked the block, and taken the twist out of the peak-halyards which I had given them when I climbed the mast off the Docking Channel; but he had also shaken the *reefs out of the jib without my permission*, consequently I made him put them both in again, which, of course, made a perfect fool of the boat, for it could hardly sail at all, without the proper balance of canvas, and I was obliged to heave-to further on and shake them out again. I made my only mistake in navigation on the way to Lowestoft; tidal errors can hardly be called mistakes, especially in the Bristol Channel, where it will take a man several years to acquire a perfect knowledge of tide. Instead of keeping in-shore, as I should have done, I passed right over what, I believe, was the Holm Sand, between a checkered black and white buoy and a red one. I did not like the appearance of the water inside, for it was so red with sand in parts as to convey the idea of being very shallow, and I knew that charts are not to be trusted implicitly for the roadstead, because of the shifting nature of the sands. The *intricacy* of the *Pilot Book* rendered an appeal to it of no *practical* use; so that, although I saw I was making for a seaway, I thought it was most likely a race of tide I had been warned about. The error was of no consequence, for there was sufficient water for me, and the seaway was not like that which breaks on an outlying sand. I had a great curiosity to see Yarmouth and Lowestoft, so that I would have stopped at them under any circumstances, for no one could surmise that Aeolus would whirl his spear a fortnight too soon, or in other words that the autumnal gales would commence so early. I paid dearly for my stoppage, and the lesson will perhaps not be lost on others, who may be anxious to make the Thames from the north.

I brought up in Lowestoft harbour in front of the band-stand, so that I had plenty of music to entertain me of an evening, as I religiously went on board every night between 8 and 9 P.M., so as to snatch a chance, if one offered; but the wind hung steadily to SW., and very strong until the 9th of September, when I crept out and beat to Southwold.

CHAPTER XIII

FROM SOUTHWOLD TO THE THAMES

THE Southwold pilots had made the little boat out a long way off; and two of them met me when about a mile above the harbour, towards which they pulled, and took up a station, as a mark for me to steer for, *The Kate* having to make sundry tacks to windward before standing in. My acquaintance with a real shingle harbour commenced at Southwold; and had I fully realised the difficulty of entering, and the great risk of being rolled over by the six-knot tide if the boat should touch, I would certainly have put one of the men on board, instead of steering in after their boat. I crossed the bar in safety, but I consider it *nothing but an absurd folly not to surrender to a pilot after the proper recognised fashion*, and would strongly advise any one to do so when dealing with a shingle-bar harbour. Southwold is a capital place for small craft, when once inside, and, as a rule, vessels can cross over the bar at two hours' flood in five or six feet.

A more secure anchorage and a more charming little watering place is not to be met with along the Norfolk or Suffolk coast.

The town lies about one mile from the harbour, the Swan Hotel offering comfortable accommodation to visitors; and the beach, or the promenade by the pilots' houses, affords a view of shipping rarely to be seen—one day presenting a fleet of four or five hundred vessels streaming out of Yarmouth and Lowestoft roads, the next (as likely as not) showing them running back, by thirties and forties at a time, before some heavy gale, while others, again, of the more obstinate sort, or better found in canvas and riding-gear, may be seen fighting it out under double reefs, until a mast is swept overboard or the sails are blown to bits. The pilots may then be seen going off as fast as launches or lifeboats will carry them, and the vessel is taken for a moderate sum, at the risk of many lives, to Lowestoft.

I was just going to breakfast with a gentleman at Southwold, on Monday, the 14th, when I saw a crowd around the lifeboat houses, which rapidly told its own tale. I crossed the river instantly, ran as hard as I could over the heavy shingle, just in time to jump into the first lifeboat I ever saw launched in my life. A seven-mile cruise lay before us, to a vessel which had its canvas blown away. A sixty-foot launch had the start of us by nearly a mile, but the lifeboat gained very considerably, and made a more weatherly course, being able to carry its full canvas, while the launch had to dip its close-reefed sail more than once. Had the chase been another three miles, or the squalls more frequent, there can be no doubt the lifeboat would have won the race; as it was, the launch obtained the prize, averaging about thirty shillings a head, at a tremendous risk of life, for it was not a morning for any but a lifeboat.

The lifeboat above mentioned carries water ballast, has a great deal of the floating power outside, and is reckoned the best lifeboat on the coast. It carries a great pressure of canvas, without which power lifeboats are not of much account. There are several mistakes made in the building of lifeboats, and I presume from the fact that their peculiar essentials are not understood. The main idea appears to have been to build a boat which would right itself if upset: such is an error, as will appear when the first essential is considered, namely, the absolute necessity for propulsion to windward in a seaway. It is almost impossible to row a lifeboat against a heavy gale and sea, so as to save life, at anything but a short distance. The boat must either sail or steam to windward, if the object of distress is a mile off. To sail, it must be masted to such an extent that it will not right itself, otherwise it cannot make the necessary weatherly course, for a lifeboat may be carried on until not a soul can stand in it; in fact, it must be able to carry a large amount of canvas when no other boat can show a rag; the oars should be a very secondary consideration. The opinion of every practical lifeboat seaman with whom I have discussed the subject is to the effect that, when a boat upsets in winter time, its crew are rendered useless by the cold, and another must be launched instantly. They one and all prefer the floating power on the outside, as it helps to pick the boat up, and allows free powerful air to support the boat inside, instead of that which loses buoyancy from being confined. No boat is as stiff as the perfectly open one, every thwart or piece of wood inside lessens the stiffness by the amount of air it displaces.

Such lifeboats as are propelled chiefly by oars should be confined to more sheltered localities, such as the Solent and the eastern part of the English Channel, for they are not fitted for the enormous rollers that break against the west and east coasts of Britain. There can be no doubt that many lives are saved with the present order of lifeboat, but the percentage will increase in the same ratio as the power of the boat to carry canvas. I am delivering not only my own opinion, but that of such men as the coxswains of the Yarmouth and Southwold lifeboats, and of numbers of practical seamen, who one and all agree that, to enable the boat to carry canvas, the gunwale should be nearly flush with the water, so that the sea will break overboard and have less to strike; the lifeboating outside, and as *high as possible*, so that the boat may sit well in the water, and keep the stern down in a seaway, so as to allow of its being steered, for if the rudder is perpetually out of water, the boat cannot be commanded. I do not know if water ballast is considered the best or not; but if it is used, there should be a number of partitions, to prevent a rush of water from one end of the boat to the other, for the neglect of such partitions has been the cause of many an upset. A drogue should form part of the equipments of all lifeboats, for they run at a tremendous pace, and are very apt to overrun the seas. "To overrun the seas" is an expression which might mean anything to the majority of readers; I will therefore explain that the high seas in a gale of wind run very fast—too fast, as a rule, for a boat; and if it is badly built, the seas will run right over it. If the boat is too fast for the seas, two dangers arise; the first, a very common one, namely, that the boat will run bows under, when the check it receives and its own pace may put it over. This is especially the case with the sea abeam, when it is an easy matter to drive about too fast. The second is of rare occurrence, and arises from a boat running faster than heavy dangerous seas, which will roll it over instantly the bow drops down into the hollow, the stern being still on top of the wave; but if the sea did not put it over in such a position, its own velocity would. Such seas are what are called "cliff seas," and are nearly as steep as a house.

I made Southwold on the 9th. Let the fate of a large vessel show what utter folly it would have been to attempt a beat round in the face of the heavy equinoctial gales. The ship passed Southwold on the 20th, in the direction of Yarmouth, having lost both anchors in the Swin after having been anchored off Southwold on the 13th. The whole navigation from the Humber into London is of the most intricate order, on account of the numerous sands which line the coast and the mouth of the Thames; also on account of the want of harbours of easy access. I was perfectly well aware, when I tripped my anchor at Wainfleet, that I had no harbour or anchorage whatever until I made Yarmouth, unless, indeed, I chose to turn tail up Boston Deeps. I look upon the run from Wainfleet as quite as risky as the passages to and from Ireland, made, as it was, on short provisions, a lee shore, and in the teeth of contrary tides, which might have swept the boat anywhere.

The new moon on September 20 gave a slight hope of more favourable weather. The flood also began to make up at an hour when some idea might be formed of the coming day. The glass is useless as a guide during continued bad weather, for the following reason. A first-rate aneroid, such as I had procured from Messrs. Beck, of Cornhill, will give about fifty-six hours' notice of bad weather; but the notice always depends upon the pace the weather is coming and the length of time it is likely to last. Thus, if the glass goes back slowly all Monday and Tuesday, a continuance of bad weather may be expected for at least three days, the widely extended atmospheric influence having been felt by the barometer at a very great distance; but when the mercury falls rapidly, a change may be expected within a few hours and will not last long, as the atmospheric influence producing the change is not widely extended, and has not been felt by the glass until comparatively close at hand. Thus it appears that on any change the weather always catches the glass up; and if storms continue for two or three weeks together, the glass works with the weather, instead of being ahead of it, and cannot be depended upon as a signal of fine weather.

The pilots were down about 4 A.M. sounding the depth on the bar, and reported that I might expect to get out at about two hours' flood. The wind was about W. by N., just favourable to Orfordness, but ahead from that point to Orford Haven or Harwich. I started about six, with two pilots on board, two of the most willing, smart little men of the very smart body of Southwold pilots; but we ran bodily aground on the bar, and *The Kate* had an uncommonly narrow escape of becoming a total wreck. The position of the shingle had no doubt changed since the men sounded at 4 A.M., and it was lucky that the boat was inside and not outside the bar, where it would have been exposed to the full force of the tide. As it was, everything depended on keeping the bow of the boat from swinging against the pier-head until a rope was made fast from the other side. I stood in the bow with a boathook firmly jammed in the pier, the violence of the pressure bending it like a fishing-rod, just allowing me to hold the bowsprit within a couple of inches of utter destruction, and threatening to hurl me over on the other side. The pilots ran the rope out to the other pier meanwhile, and the boat was eventually in safety.

> Postquam altos tetigit fluctus, et ad aequora venit—
> [When through the surf and on the open sea]—*Æn*. iii. 662.

I made Orford Haven just at tide-time, and was put in by a fisherman from a smack. A shifting shingle bar makes a pilot always a necessity, as at Southwold. The haven faces to the south, so that the entrance cannot be seen by one approaching from the north until it has been passed.

I made Harwich on the next day, September 22, and determined to wait for a wind before attempting to find my way through the various sands that make the entrance into, and the navigation of, the Thames so intricate. There is not a more difficult place in the world for a stranger to find than the passage between the Gunfleet and the Buxey Sands. There are usually a number of craft going through; but it would be absurd to follow any particular craft, unless quite certain of the course it is steering, for there are numberless other places it may be going to. The land to starboard is no guide to the stranger, except the wind be NW., for if SE. (as I had it) the land must be left nearly out of sight and the Gunfleet kept aboard. One miserable buoy marks the channel to the north, and another to the south. The north buoy should be a lightship visible for miles in clear weather.

The Kate at anchor in the Thames, off the Maplin. Gale of wind. Time about 6 P.M.

I steered a compass course from the Naze to the buoy, but very soon found that was all moonshine, as the tide set me towards the land, compelling me to haul out again and speak a brig that had come through the swashway, and which put me in a fair line for it. I passed about a quarter of a mile east of the buoys, and found myself fairly in the Thames, where I had fully intended to make fast to the first steamer I could get hold of, unless the wind favoured my run up. The breeze held at SE., and I was content (for the first time during the voyage) to follow others, instead of using my own sense as to the best course.

I passed close to the Maplin light, and then hauled up a little, as I saw others doing; but in truth I should have steered about two points higher, well to windward of the Mouse light, which should have been left as close as possible on the port-hand. I passed nearly three-quarters of a mile to leeward, being in fact on the Maplin Sand before I discovered that the tide had set me there. The consequence was, I had to haul much closer to the wind, and had only just got clear of the sand and was well down in the bight, when, being caught in a heavy thunderstorm, I brought up without a moment's hesitation about 200 yards from the Maplin black buoy.

> Haec ubi dicta, cavum conversa cuspide montem
> Impulit in latus; ac venti, velut agmine facto,
> Qua data porta, ruunt, et terras turbine perflant.
> Incubuere mari, totumque a sedibus imis
> Una Eurusque Notusque ruunt, creberque procellis
> Africus, et vastos volvunt ad litora fluctus.
> Insequitur clamorque virum stridorque rudentum.
> Eripiunt subito nubes coelumque diemque
> Teucrorum ex oculis: ponto nox incubat atra:
> Intonuere poli, et crebris micat ignibus aether;
> Praesentemque viris intentant omnia mortem.—*Æneidos* i. 81–91.

TRANSLATION.

> He answered, whirled his spear, and struck the cave.
> The tempests rush, in mass, o'er land and wave,
> From south and east and rough south-west, and speed,
> As whirlwinds follow gales, as each succeed,
> To quiver ocean's depths: awake the shore
> With mighty billows' lash: resounding roar.
> Men shout; the cordage creaks; and darkness reigns;
> The thunders crash; reflash the lightning's chains—
> All nature threats with death, as if, indeed,
> The heavens bowed to crush the earthly seed.

Such was the storm which raged for some two hours, and rendered it almost impossible for me to light any one of the lamps, for the cloud of fine rain baffles description. It was in a great measure the rebound of the heavy rain that was falling all round, and was driven along just like the spray from the fountains at the Crystal Palace, only with the thickness of a mist and at great speed. I was wet through long before I had stowed all my sails, but never knew until that night how much water a straw hat will hold. My last action on leaving the Pier Hotel at Harwich was to buy another box of matches, in addition to those on board. A perfect deluge of water from my straw hat completely did for it, but the mere fact of touching the striker with a wet hand would have been quite sufficient. I first of all attempted to light the binnacle, from which I might hope to light the rest; but after wasting a large number of the best wax matches, and becoming alarmed for the remainder, I desisted and crept underneath the main-hatch, where I found everything in a miserable state of dampness, but where, after another serious expenditure of matches, I was lucky enough to light the riding lamp, from it the port and starboard lights, and from them the binnacle.

It blew hard from the south throughout the night; but as long as the cable held and the lights burned, there was no immediate danger. I thought once or twice of shifting my anchorage before dark, because I was in the track of every description of vessel; but to do so, I must have run back to the Mouse light, and that was almost impossible as the wind was. I therefore stayed where I was, although by working back I would have secured the assistance of the tug-steamer I had passed on my way, which was at anchor off the Mouse the last thing at dusk and the first thing in the morning, from which I argue it was there all night.

The novelty of the position was delightful, though I would have preferred some dry clothes, for it was rather cold, in spite of the lifebelt, which I put on for the last time during the voyage, and a large railway rug, which I wrapped around greatcoat and lifebelt, giving my upper proportions a very imposing appearance. The strong breeze knocked up a very nasty sea in the tideway and made it very dangerous work travelling the deck, for the boat lay for some hours of tide right in the trough, and rolled tremendously. My rounds were made every hour up to eleven and after 2 A.M.; but between those hours I slept quite soundly in the well, making the discovery, for the first time, that it was very nicely suited to my length when sitting with my back against the side and protected above by the forward half of the hatches. The particular points to be observed were:—No. 1: To kneel down securely in the bow, and hold the cable in the right hand until it tightened like a bar of iron, and showed that the anchor was holding; the process is very apt to jerk a clumsy man overboard, but it should always be done when it is so dark that you cannot satisfy yourself with eyesight that she is not dragging. No. 2: To examine the chafing-gear, and take particular care of that which plays against the bobstay; the boat's head should be carefully watched, and the rudder be set so as to keep it from chafing the rope cable against the stay; the chain cable and big anchor should be held in reserve, for it is sometimes very difficult, if not impossible, for one hand to recover it in the strong tide and deep water of the Thames. No. 3: To examine and retrim the port and starboard lights. To retrim either light requires a journey forward to fetch it, when a firm grip must be taken of the rigging while the light is being unshipped, otherwise the heavy rolling will jerk the unfortunate overboard. The light must be taken down to the well when unshipped: cleaned, filled with oil, and another journey forward must replace it, when, if the other one wants trimming, it can be brought at the saving of a journey. The mainboom should be well lashed on such occasions, as it is a grand thing to hold on by; but such lashing should be looked to, for everything has a tendency to work loose in a seaway. I was very nearly knocked overboard by the swing of the mainboom, which unfortunately worked loose, on one of my return passages. Yachtsmen generally stow the peak separately from the boom; but practical seamen always make one stow and lash the two firmly together. No. 4: To trim the riding and binnacle light. The riding light had to be trimmed a number of times, as an unfortunate mistake had been made in furnishing the candles, the largest supply being unsuited to the purpose, burning great cauliflower-looking wicks, and lasting only a few hours.

The night was of the darkest, and I kept watch till about 8 P.M., when I rolled myself up snugly in the well, and bestowed occasional peeps on passing steamers or other craft. The steamers from the Swin Channel that I saw, and I saw an immense number, steered straight on to *The Kate*; some of them yawed frantically with their lights, as a challenge to me, I presume; for my port and starboard lights naturally led many to suppose I was under weigh. They one and all kept a first-rate

The Kate at anchor in the Thames. Night pitch dark. Vessels' lights in all directions. Time: midnight.

look-out, and diverged to the right or left, but the greater number passed my port bow within speaking distance and several of them offered me a tow.

I awoke from a sound sleep at 2 A.M., just in time to save all the lights from expiring. The riding light had been a curiosity of glass tenacity for about a month, for there was no proper fixture for it, and the glass had cracked in many ways, owing to the deflection of the flame, so much so that I would not allow the waterman at Harwich to attempt to clean it. How it held out through the night was astonishing, considering the frantic manner in which it swung round and round the nearly vertical stay, as far as the lanyard would permit, and then returned with like vigour. I tried various lashings, but only a vertical fastening to the deck would have answered, and that was impossible. I kept it on the mizenstay, in preference to the forestay, because, if on the forestay, the width of the mast might possibly have hid it from a steamer coming astern, and it was an absolute necessity as a stern light, for the port and starboard lights could not be seen further aft than the beam.

The flood tide made up at 3 A.M., a very unfortunate hour for me, because, jammed as I was so close to the Maplin, I had to wait for daylight before I could trip the anchor. I had hoisted the pilot jack shortly after bringing-up on the previous evening, and for the first time neglected to take down the flag bearing the boat's name, but fastened the jack underneath—an egregious error, as will be seen. I commenced operations about 5.30, set the mainsail with a reef in it, and reefed the jib, for the weather looked anything but promising. I had paid out from twenty-five to thirty fathoms of rope, and never had a harder job than to get the anchor on that particular occasion. The mere strength of any one man would have been thrown away, without a proper manœuvring of the canvas. The mainsail must have been set, or the boat could not be commanded on the tripping of the anchor, but the effect of the mainsail was to place the boat's head at right angles with the anchor, rendering it almost impossible to gain one inch of rope. I hoisted the jib, and brought the sheet to windward; but that did not answer, as the head still maintained a great angle with the cable. I then shipped the tiller, put it hard up, eased off the mainsheet, and sailed her clean over the anchor, rounding in the cable as fast as ever I could. A turn round the bits, a jump aft to let go the jib-halyards and put the tiller amidships, enabled me to lift the anchor with ease as the tide drifted the boat over it for the second time, but within a yard or two of the Maplin black buoy, before the anchor was on board, the jib set, and the boat under full command, shortly after 6 A.M.

The wind was dead ahead; but had I known the river, the remaining three hours' tide would have taken me to Southend, for I am under the impression that I could have cut across the Maplin at that time of tide. However, being a perfect stranger to the river, I determined to get well up to windward, for fear the wind should go to the N. of W., which might be reckoned on towards twelve o'clock. A tug-steamer was lying at anchor where I had seen it on the previous evening, a few miles to windward, and I set to work to beat up towards it, in the hopes of getting a tow. The afternoon tide made up so late, the days darkened so quickly, and the weather was so uncertain, that another night in the Thames might have ended in my being blown out to sea again, even if I escaped being run down from a want of lights. The riding light could not have been hoisted, as one of the cracked pieces of glass had fallen out, an accident I discovered after bringing up the second time, and put the lamp out, as another piece might have fallen out and set the boat on fire—for, not trusting a single match on board, I had kept the candle lit, the binnacle and other lamps requiring to be cleaned and trimmed before they could be used again.

I had been working to windward for about an hour and a half when the thunder-clouds banked up so heavily that I expected a squall every minute, and became aware that if called on to lower the mainsail in a hurry, the pilot flag would be certain to catch in all three blocks and render the lowering of the sail impossible. The sharp lessons I had been taught by the masthead flag jamming the peak halyard-block caused me to bring up instantly, and climb the mast to remove the flag and rehoist it properly. But the smoke from the steamers at Harwich had made all the ropes more or less greasy, and the signal-halyards worse than the rest, so that I failed to untie the knot, and was about to cut away the whole concern, when the bright idea struck me that I might fasten the deck end of the halyards high up in the mizen rigging, and thus cause the flag to fly out quite clear of the blocks. I slid down, and acted accordingly; the flags blew out as I had expected; whether the halyards would or would not interfere with the peak of the mainsail, I determined should be settled next tide, if necessary; for I fully expected a tow from the tug which was riding at anchor about a mile off, or some of the others which were passing up and down the river. But none of them took the slightest notice, either of my flag, the waving of my yachting cap, or the firing of my revolver; and had it not been for the kind assistance of the captain of a commercial steamer who unexpectedly offered me a tow, I might have been run down, either when attempting Sheerness or riding at anchor without the proper lights up. *The Kate* was then lying about a mile west of one of the Ouze Sand buoys, and to windward of some red buoys, which, I imagine, must have been some on the Maplin Sand. The *Pilot Book* marks all the Maplin buoys as black; in fact, the confusion caused by the removal of buoys and their change of colour is one of the difficulties of Thames navigation, and it would be useless for me to attempt to define the exact water in which I was anchored.

I got my anchor up, and the steamer hove me a rope, which I made fast, but I was so anxious to prevent it chafing the jib that, instead of jumping aft to the tiller, I seized the oar to bear the bow off the steamer's side; it slipped, crash went the bowsprit, and *The Kate* was a wreck at last. The boathook was, unfortunately, on the other side of the deck, or it would have saved the spar. The steamer had been brought alongside of my boat in the most clever manner, and no accident occurred on that account, but after I had fastened on their tow-rope it had not been slacked away sufficiently before one unfortunate turn was given to the screw propeller. The steamer forged ahead before I could drop astern, and thus the accident happened. The spar broke very badly, so that it was impossible to splice it, but a fish was made at Gravesend by binding some pieces of iron along the broken part.

Et sylvis aptare trabes, et stringere remos (*Æneidos* i. 553).
[And choose the shoots to bind along the oars.]

The bowsprit in that state would not reeve through the hole made for it, but had to be lashed on top of the bits and over the rail, so that the jib would not sit on it other than reefed; but the general appearance of the boat was improved by this, the jib (when stowed along) hiding the fracture from ordinary observation.

I left the boat for the night in charge at the Victoria Dock, and it was taken up to the builders' yard the next day.

ITINERARY

1869 June 15 Limehouse–Greenhithe
16 Greenhithe–Ramsgate
18 Ramsgate–Folkestone
19 Folkestone–Rye
21 Rye–Hastings
22 Hastings–Eastbourne
23 Eastbourne–Brighton
24–25 Brighton–Littlehampton–Selsea Bill–Calshot
25 Calshot–Southampton
30 Southampton–Hurst–Swanage–Weymouth

July 1 Weymouth–Portland Bill–Bridport–Lyme Regis
2 Lyme–Torquay
5 Torquay–Dartmouth
9 Dartmouth–Salcombe
10 Salcombe–Plymouth
11 Plymouth–Falmouth
12 Falmouth–Coverack
13 Coverack–Penzance
14 Penzance–Sennen Cove (Land's End)
15 Sennen Cove–St. Ives
17 St. Ives–Newquay
19 Newquay–Padstow
20 Padstow–Boscastle
21–22 Boscastle–Lundy
23 Lundy–Milford
27 Milford–Dale Roads
28 Dale Roads–Skomer Island
30–31 Skomer–Courtown

Aug. 2 Courtown–Wicklow
3 Wicklow–Kingstown
5 Kingstown–Howth–The Skerries
6 The Skerries–Ardglass
7 Ardglass–Donaghadee
13 Donaghadee–Ayr
14–15 Ayr–Irvine–Greenock–Bowling
15–17 Crinan Canal–Bowling–Grangemouth
18 Grangemouth–Leith
19 Leith–Cockenzie
20 Cockenzie–Dunbar
21 Dunbar–North Sunderland
22 Sunderland–Boulmer
23–24 Boulmer–Tynemouth
25–26 Tynemouth–Hartlepool
26 Hartlepool–Whitby

164

ITINERARY